New perspectives on economic development

New perspectives on economic development

A human agency approach

Fu-Lai Tony Yu

Wageningen Academic
Publishers

ISBN: 978-90-8686-160-6
e-ISBN: 978-90-8686-716-5
DOI: 10.3920/978-90-8686-716-5

First published, 2011

Preface and acknowledgments

This book puts together 10 papers in human agency economics while the author taught economic development and entrepreneurship at Feng Chia University (Taiwan) and Shue Yan University (Hong Kong). Chapter 1 reviews theories of economic development in history of Austrian economics, with the intention of extending the contributions of major Austrian economists to development phenomena. After pointing out the weaknesses in the orthodox neoclassical approach to economic growth, Chapter 2 introduces a subjectivist approach to understand issues in economic development. Specifically, it utilizes theories of human agency to interpret economic phenomena and policies. It also serves as a methodological foundation for arguments elaborated in the next seven chapters. Chapters 3 to 9 respectively discuss important issues in economic development, namely, entrepreneurial process, national capabilities, innovation, trade, government, transition and catching up strategies for firms in latecomer economies. Chapter 10 provides a concluding remark and proposes a new agenda for research in economic development. Earlier versions of some chapters in this book were previously presented at international conferences and/or published in academic journals. I thank conference participants for their comments and acknowledge the publishers of the following journals for permission to reproduce some materials in this volume.

Part of material in Chapter 2 is published in 'A subjectivist approach to strategic management', *Managerial and Decision Economics*, special issue: 'integrating management and economic perspectives on corporate strategy', volume 24 (40), June 2003, pp. 335-345; I thank the guest editors of the special issue, J. Rajendran Pandian and Paul L. Robertson for their generous comments. The article is reprinted in I. Nonaka (editor) *Knowledge Management: Critical Perspectives on Business and Management*, London, UK: Routledge Falmer, pp. 298-314.

Chapter 3 is modified from paper, 'A dynamic model of the entrepreneurial process: a human agency perspective', presented at the International Conference on 'Business and information', 11-13 July 2007, Tokyo, Japan. The article is published in *International Journal of Innovation and Learning*, volume 6 (3), 2009, pp. 285-305.

Chapter 4 is based on 'National capabilities and economic development: a subjectivist view', paper presented at the conference: 'Knowledge and economic and social change: new challenges to innovation studies', 7-9 April 2003, organized by Advances in the Economic and Social Analysis of Technology and the Institute of Innovation Research held in Manchester School of Management Building, Manchester, United Kingdom. The article is published in *Forum for Development Studies*, volume 3 (2), 2003, pp. 247-267.

Chapter 5 (Innovation and communication) is adapted from 'Novelty and its acceptance: an inter-subjective perspective', *International Journal of Arts and Technology*, volume 1 (1), 2008, pp. 119-130. An earlier version of this paper was presented at the International Conference on 'Knowledge-based economy and global management' held on 6-7 December 2007, College of Management, Southern Taiwan University of Technology (Taiwan). It also receives 'The Best Conference Paper Award' in the 5th multi-disciplinary management conference on 'Creativity and enterprising' organized by Department of Business Administration, Tung Hai University (Taiwan), 26 April 2008.

Chapter 6 is adapted from 'A human agency approach to economics of international trade', *International Journal of Pluralism and Economic Education*, volume 1 (1/2), October 2009, pp. 22-36.

Chapter 7 is rewritten from 'Uncertainty, human agency and e-government', *Transforming Government: People, Process and Policy*, volume 2 (4), 2008, pp. 283-296.

Chapter 8 is based on 'Toward a subjective perspective of transition', paper presented at the international conference, 'Evolution of institutions and the knowledge economy', organized by the University of Debrecen held at Debrecen, Hungary (4-5 October 2002). The article is published in *Philippines Journal of Development*, volume 30 (2), 2003, pp. 255-275.

Part of material in Chapter 10 is based on my work with Dr. Gary Moon Cheung Shiu (2009), 'The Austrian school of economics', unpublished working paper.

As mentioned, this volume is a collection of papers written over the past several years. Each of the individual papers has consistently applied the Austrian subjectivist framework to economic and development issues. Since a new idea does not arise from a vacuum, but builds upon previous ideas, when individual papers are gathered into a book form, some materials/ arguments will be unavoidably repeated. In preparing this volume, every effort is made to avoid repetition while at the same time ensuring that the arguments in each chapter flow smoothly without a loss of continuity. I extend my apology for some repetition of materials, if any. I have enjoyed and benefited from stimulating discussion with my academic friends, Teresa Shan-Yu Chen, Simon Chien-Yuan Chen, Dian Kwan, Gary Moon-Cheung Shiu, Ho-don Yan, and scholars from the Chinese Hayek Society over the past years. I am very grateful to Dian Kwan for her proofreading of the earlier drafts of individual papers. Of course, none of them bears any responsibility for the errors or shortcomings in this volume.

Fu-Lai Tony Yu

Professor
Department of Economics and Finance
Hong Kong Shue Yan University
Email: flyu@hksyu.edu

Table of contents

Chapter 1.
Economic development in Austrian economics

1.1 Introduction: economic development in Austrian economics

Since its founding father Carl Menger published *Principle of Economics* in 1871, the Austrian school of economics focuses their analysis on areas such as exchange and market process, the structure of production, entrepreneurship, business cycle, monetary theories, economic calculation and central planning[1] (for example, see topics discussed by Von Mises 1949/1963 and Shand 1984, and articles included in classic collections in Littlechild 1990 and Kirzner 1994). However, major Austrian economists mention little about, if not entirely neglect, economic development.[2] Having said that, it is still possible to pick up the arguments on economic development discussed in the works of Carl Menger, Eugene von Bohm-Bawerk, Ludwig von Mises, Fredrick A. Hayek and Israel M. Kirzner. Since Carl Menger introduced knowledge problems and entrepreneurship in *Principle of Economics* in 1871, the two elements have become the tenets of Austrian economics. It is probably no exaggeration to claim that any advance in the Austrian model of economic development would be impossible if the twin notions of knowledge and entrepreneurship have not been placed on the forefront of the analysis. In what follows, we shall review major Austrian scholars' works on economic development, with the intention of generating a rudiment Austrian theory of economic development.

1.2 Carl Menger: uncertainty, knowledge and entrepreneurship

Menger starts the discussion of economic development by introducing Adam Smith's famous division of labor. Menger (1871/1994: 72-74) writes:

---

[1] The Austrian school of economics does not discuss economics of innovation, though there is a theory of entrepreneurial discovery.

[2] The term economic development or economic progress is not indexed in Von Mises' *Human Action* (1949/1963).

> 'The greatest improvement in the productive powers of labour', says Adam Smith, 'and the greater part of the skill, dexterity, and judgment with which it is anywhere directed, or applied, seem to have been the effects of the division of labour'. And: 'It is the great multiplication of the productions of all the different arts, in consequence of the division of labour, which occasions, in a well-governed society, that universal opulence which extends itself to the lowest ranks of the people'.

Acknowledging Smith's contribution, Menger argues that other, but important, causes of economic progress have escaped Smith's attention. This is through the production of higher order goods.[3] As Menger introduces:

> 'Assume a people which extends its attention to goods of third, fourth, and higher orders, instead of confining its activity merely to the tasks of a primitive collecting economy – that is, to the acquisition of naturally available goods of lowest order (ordinarily goods of first, and possibly second, order). If such a people progressively directs goods of ever higher orders to the satisfaction of its needs, and especially if each step in this direction is accompanied by an appropriate division of labor, we shall doubtless observe that progress in welfare which Adam Smith was disposed to attribute exclusively to the latter factor. We shall see the hunter, who initially pursues game with a club, turning to hunting with bow and hunting net, to stock farming of the simplest kind, and in sequence, to ever more intensive forms of stock farming. We shall see men, living initially on wild plants, turning to ever more intensive forms of agriculture. We shall see the rise of manufactures, and their improvement by means of tools and machines. And in the closest connection with these developments, we shall see the welfare of this people increase'.

The argument of using goods of higher order to produce goods of lower order anticipates Von Bohm-Bawerk's roundabout production process. Furthermore, Menger alludes the act of combining higher order goods to produce lower order goods for more future consumption with human knowledge and entrepreneurship. This paves way for insightful analyses

[3] Menger (1871/1994: 56-67) classifies economic goods into two types, goods of lower order (consumption goods) and goods of higher order (means of production). In production, goods of higher order are to be combined together to produce goods of lower order.

furthered by Von Mises, Hayek and Kirzner. In Menger's words (Menger 1871/1994: 74):

> 'if men abandon this most primitive form of economy, investigate the ways in which things may be combined in a causal process for the production of consumption goods, take possession of things capable of being so combined, and treat them as goods of higher order, they will obtain consumption goods that are as truly the results of natural processes as the consumption goods of a primitive collecting economy, but the available quantities of these goods will no longer be independent of the wishes and needs of men. Instead, the quantities of consumption goods will be determined by a process that is in the power of men and is regulated by human purposes within the limits set by natural laws. Consumption goods, which before were the product of an accidental concurrence of the circumstances of their origin, become products of human will, within the limits set by natural laws, as soon as men have *recognized* these circumstances and have achieved control of them. *The quantities of consumption goods at human disposal are limited only by the extent of human knowledge of the causal connections between things, and by the extent of human control over these things.* Increasing understanding of the causal connections between things and human welfare, and increasing control of the less proximate conditions responsible for human welfare, have led mankind, therefore, from a state of barbarism and the deepest misery to its present stage of civilization and well-being.... Nothing is more certain than that the degree of economic progress of mankind will still, in future epochs, be commensurate with the degree of progress of human knowledge' [italics added].

Menger is probably the first economist to acknowledge the significance of time and error in economic activities. Due to uncertainty, entrepreneurs play four major roles on economic development. Menger (1871/1994: 159-161) argues:

> 'The process of transforming goods of higher order into goods of lower or first order, provided it is economic in other respects, must also always be *planned and conducted, with some economic purpose in view, by an economizing individual.* This individual must carry through the economic computations ... and he must actually bring the goods of higher order, including technical labor services, together ...

> for the purpose of production.... An entrepreneur ... makes not only the underlying economic calculations but also the actual decisions to assign goods of higher order to particular productive purposes. Entrepreneurial activity includes: (a) obtaining information about the economic situation; (b) economic calculation – all the various computations that must be made if a production process is to be efficient (provided that it is economic in other respects); (c) the act of will by which goods of higher order (or goods in general – under conditions of developed commerce, where any economic good can be exchanged for any other) are assigned to a particular production process; and finally (d) supervision of the execution of the production plan so that it may be carried through as economically as possible'.

Menger points out that the values of factors of production come from the value individuals place on the final product or consumers' good, which amounts to a backward imputation of value for those factors. In other words, 'consumer sovereignty' ultimately determines not only the prices of consumers' goods, but also the prices of all factors of production (Anderson 2001). Since then, the view that consumer sovereignty directing the production of final goods and economic development has become an Austrian tradition.[4]

In conclusion, Menger's classification of goods paves way for Von Bohm-Bawerk to formulate his capital theory. Menger's emphasis on time, knowledge problems and the importance of entrepreneurship in economic development has become the central focus of the Austrian school of economics.

1.3 Eugene von Bohm-Bawerk: the roundabout production process in the capitalist development

In *Capital and Interest,* Von Bohm-Bawerk (1890: Bk.II, Ch.III, par.52)[5] argues that 'progressive economical development, which is simply man's progressive mastery over nature, enables man to replace the goods he

[4] In Von Mises' view (1949/1963), 'consumer sovereignty' individuals who purchase goods and services in a free market 'are at the helm and steer the ship'. 'The consumers determine ultimately not only the prices of the consumers' goods, but no less the prices of all factors of production'. Simply put, the choices of consumers will ultimately determine the choices of producers (Anderson 2001). See also Gunning (2009).

[5] Citations from Von Bohm-Bawerk's works are based on the version posted at 'Library of Economics and Liberty' website, http: //www.econlib.org/library/BohmBawerk/bbPTC.html.

needs at a steadily decreasing cost'. This progress manifests in taking a roundabout process in production. As Holcombe (1998: 45-62) correctly argues that Von Bohm-Bawerk 'depicts a structure of production that would become more roundabout as more indirect methods of production were used. Von Bohm-Bawerk's ideas about heterogeneous capital and more roundabout methods of production have remained an integral part of Austrian capital theory ... and illuminate the process of economic growth'.

As mentioned above, Menger's emphasis on two types of goods, namely goods of lower order and goods of higher order in the structure of production anticipates Von Bohm-Bawerk's capital theory. Economic development, in Von Bohm-Bawerk's view, is the result of capital investment which takes on a roundabout production method. In his *Positive Theory of Capital,* Von Bohm-Bawerk (1891: Bk.I, Ch.II, par.1) introduces the concept of roundabout production method:

> 'The end and aim of all production is the making of things with which to satisfy our wants ... We either put forth our labour just before the goal is reached, or we, intentionally, take a roundabout way. That is to say, we may put forth our labour in such a way that it at once completes the circle of conditions necessary for the emergence of the desired good, and thus the existence of the good *immediately* follows the expenditure of the labour; or we may associate our labour first with the more remote causes of the good, with the object of obtaining, not the desired good itself, but a proximate cause of the good; which cause, again, must be associated with other suitable materials and powers, till, finally, – perhaps through a considerable number of intermediate members, – the finished good, the instrument of human satisfaction, is obtained'.

Von Bohm-Bawerk (1891: Bk.I, Ch.II, par.3) illustrates his notion of the roundabout process in water supply activity:

> 'A peasant requires drinking water. The spring is some distance from his house. There are various ways in which he may supply his daily wants. First, he may go to the spring each time he is thirsty, and drink out of his hollowed hand. This is the most direct way; satisfaction follows immediately on exertion. But it is an inconvenient way, for our peasant has to take his way to the well as often as he is thirsty. And it is an insufficient way, for he can never collect and store any great quantity such as he requires for various other purposes. Second, he

> may take a log of wood, hollow it out into a kind of pail, and carry his day's supply from the spring to his cottage. The advantage is obvious, but it necessitates a roundabout way of considerable length. The man must spend, perhaps, a day in cutting out the pail; before doing so he must have felled a tree in the forest; to do this, again, he must have made an axe, and so on. But there is still a third way; instead of felling one tree he fells a number of trees, splits and hollows them, lays them end for end, and so constructs a runnel or rhone which brings a full head of water to his cottage. Here, obviously, between the expenditure of the labour and the obtaining of the water we have a very roundabout way, but, then, the result is ever so much greater. Our peasant needs no longer take his weary way from house to well with the heavy pail on his shoulder, and yet he has a constant and full supply of the freshest water at his very door'.

Hence, Von Bohm-Bawark (1891: Bk I, Ch.II, par.6-7) concludes 'that a greater result is obtained by producing goods in roundabout ways than by producing them directly. Where a good can be produced in either way, it is the fact that, by the indirect way, a greater product can be got with equal labour, or the same product with less labour. But, beyond this, the superiority of the indirect way manifests itself in being the only way in which certain goods can be obtained; if I might say so, it is so much the better that it is often the only way! ... That roundabout methods lead to greater results than direct methods is one of the most important and fundamental propositions in the whole theory of production'. Furthermore, 'every roundabout way means the enlisting in our service of a power which is stronger or more cunning than the human hand; every extension of the roundabout way means an addition to the powers which enter into the service of man, and the shifting of some portion of the burden of production from the scarce and costly labour of human beings to the prodigal powers of nature' (Von Bohm-Bawark 1891: Bk.I, Ch.II, par.9). However, whether the roundabout process will be taken depends on two factors, namely, means of subsistence and profitability of the process. Von Bohm-Bawark (1891: Bk.I, Ch.V, par.27) notes:

> 'The way of capitalist production is long and roundabout, and man cannot enter upon it unless he is provided with the means of subsistence for the time that must intervene before he reaps the return. But it is ... not the means of subsistence alone, that constitutes capital. Capital only comes into existence when man actually enters upon the profitable roundabout journey that the

means of subsistence have made possible; when he builds machines, tools, railways, factories, raises raw materials, and so on. However abundant the means of subsistence were, if the workers were to consume them in living from hand to mouth, the community would evidently never accumulate capital at all'.

According to Von Bohm-Bawerk, there are advantage and disadvantage of adopting capitalist methods of production. The advantage consists in the greater technical productiveness of those methods. With an equal amount of primary productive powers, more or better goods can be produced by a better chosen capitalist process than direct unassisted production. The disadvantage connected with the capitalist method of production is its sacrifice of time. The roundabout ways of capital are fruitful but long; they present us more or better consumption goods, but only at a later period of time (Von Bohm-Bawark 1891: Bk.II, Ch.II, par.10-11).

Von Bohm-Bawark's capital theory raises many controversies in history of economics. This is not the scope of the present study to go into detail of the debates.[6] Perhaps, Lachmann's remark (1978: 79) is worth noting, 'we must try to see Von Bohm-Bawerk's thesis in its proper setting. Like Adam Smith's division of labour ... the principle of roundabout production is, correctly interpreted, a theorem about economic progress'.

[6] Moss (1976: 56-57) summarizes the debate as follows: 'There is some disagreement in the literature on the degree to which Von Bohm-Bawerk in fact allowed productivity considerations to enter his theory. The issue goes back at least to Frank A. Fetter's remark in 1902 that it "has been a surprise to many students of Von Bohm-Bawerk to find that he has presented a theory, the most prominent feature of which is the technical productiveness of roundabout processes. His criticism of the productivity theories of interest has been of such a nature as to lead to the belief that he utterly rejected them ... [But] it appears from Bohm-Bawerk's later statement that he does not object to the productivity theory as a partial, but as an exclusive, explanation of interest". Much later Schumpeter insisted that productivity plays only a subsidiary role in what is in fact wholly a time-preference theory. It is of some interest to note that when Bohm-Bawerk considered the alternative roles for productivity in a time-conscious theory, he came out squarely for an interpretation that placed productivity and "impatience" on the same level. Bohm-Bawerk made it very clear that he was not willing to identify his position with that of Fetter, who espoused a time-preference theory of interest without any mention of productivity considerations. Bohm-Bawerk remarked that "Fetter himself espouses a [theory which] places him on the outer-most wing of the purely 'psychological' interest theorists – 'psychological' as opposed to 'technical'. He moves into a position far more extreme than the one I occupy ...".

1.4 Ludwig von Mises: entrepreneurship, economic calculation and the market process

While Von Bohm-Bawerk constructs a theory of capital based on Menger's classification of goods of first order and higher orders, Von Mises introduces the entrepreneur who conducts economic calculation for the capital deplored in the production process. In *Human Action*, Von Mises (1949/1963: 301) claims, 'the marvelous economic improvements of the last two hundred years were an achievement of the capitalists who provided the capital goods required and of the elite of technologists and entrepreneurs'. Furthermore, Von Mises (1949/1963: 297) argues,

> 'The vehicle of economic progress is the accumulation of additional capital goods by means of saving and improvement in technological methods of production the execution of which is almost always conditioned by the availability of such new capital. The agents of progress are the promoting entrepreneurs intent upon profiting by means of adjusting the conduct of affairs to the best possible satisfaction of the consumers ... An excess of the total amount of profits over that of losses is a proof of the fact that there is economic progress and an improvement in the standard of living of all strata of the population. The greater this excess is, the greater is the increment in general prosperity'.

Entrepreneurs in the market are guided by the signals of profit and losses which is ultimately related to consumers' tastes and preferences. As Von Mises (1949/1963: 299) argues,

> 'The entrepreneurial function, the striving of entrepreneurs after profits, is the driving power in the market economy. Profit and loss are the devices by means of which the consumers exercise their supremacy on the market. The behavior of the consumers makes profits and losses appear and thereby shifts ownership of the means of production from the hands of the less efficient into those of the more efficient. It makes a man the more influential in the direction of business activities the better he succeeds in serving the consumers. In the absence of profit and loss the entrepreneurs would not know what the most urgent needs of the consumers are. If some entrepreneurs were to guess it, they would lack the means to adjust production accordingly. Profit-seeking business is subject

> to the sovereignty of the consumers, while non-profit institutions are sovereign unto themselves and not responsible to the public. Production for profit is necessarily production for use, as profits can only be earned by providing the consumers with those things they most urgently want to use'.

Von Mises is in strong defense of private property for economic progress. Von Mises (1922/1981) argues that the great progress in this sphere of economic life has been achieved by private enterprise. Von Mises' critique of socialist system is best summarized by Boettke (2005: 1)[7] as follows,

> '[Von Mises] emphasized not only the incentives that individuals face in the context of private property versus collective property arrangements, but the functional significance of clearly defined and enforced property rights for the economic calculation of alternative investment opportunities. Without a clear notion of "mine" and "thine", the institutional basis for exchange is lost. Without exchange relationships, monetary prices will not be formed on the market. Without money prices upon which to compare and contrast prospective employments of scarce resources, profit and loss signals will not be able to guide adjustments to resource use'.

Von Mises' (1949/1963: 808-9) opposition of government intervention and any form of taxation can be clearly seen in the following messages:

> 'Confiscatory taxation results in checking economic progress and improvement not only by its effect upon capital accumulation. It brings about a general trend toward stagnation and the preservation of business practices which could not last under the competitive conditions of the unhampered market economy ... But today taxes often absorb the greater part of the newcomer's "excessive" profits. He cannot accumulate capital; he cannot expand his own business; he will never become big business and a match for the vested interests. The old firms do not need to fear his competition; they are sheltered by the tax collector. They may with impunity indulge in routine, they may defy the wishes of the public and become conservative. It is true, the income tax prevents them, too, from accumulating new capital. But what is more important for them is that it prevents the dangerous newcomer from accumulating any capital. They are

[7] In this message, Boettke also refers to F.A. Hayek.

virtually privileged by the tax system. In this sense progressive taxation checks economic progress and makes for rigidity. While under unhampered capitalism the ownership of capital is a liability forcing the owner to serve the consumers, modern methods of taxation transform it into a privilege.

1.5 Friedrick A. Hayek: competition, discovery process and spontaneous growth

In the Mengerian tradition, Hayek argues that due to human ignorance, the growth of civilization is the *unintended* consequence of human's economizing action. Hayek is a strong advocate of spontaneous order. Hayek (1952/1979: 150) notes:

> 'Though our civilization is the result of a cumulation of individual knowledge, it is not by the explicit or conscious combination of all this knowledge in any individual brain, but by its embodiment in symbols which we use without understanding them ... Many of the greatest things man has achieved are the result not of consciously directed thought, and still less the product of a deliberately coordinated effort of many individuals, but of a process in which the individual plays a part which he can never fully understand.'

Elsewhere, he (Hayek 1968) argues, 'our civilization is indeed largely an unforeseen and unintended outcome of our submitting to moral and legal rules which were never "invented" with such a result in mind, but which grew because those societies which developed them piecemeal prevailed at every step over other groups which followed different rules, less conducive to the growth of civilization.'

1.5.1 Knowledge problems in the process of economic change

Hayek links economic problems with knowledge problems and 'economic problems arise always and only in consequence of change' (Hayek 1949: 82). Hayek (1949) emphasizes one kind of knowledge which is particularly relevant for coordination problems. This kind of 'unorganized knowledge which cannot possibly be called scientific in the sense of knowledge of general rules: the knowledge of the particular circumstances of time and place'. Hayek (1949: 77) explains the significance of dispersed knowledge in economic progress as follows,

> 'The peculiar character of the problem of a rational economic order is determined precisely by the fact that the knowledge of the circumstances of which we must make use never exists in concentrated or integrated form but solely as the dispersed bits of incomplete and frequently contradictory knowledge which all the separate individuals possess. The economic problem of society is thus not merely a problem of how to allocate "given" resources – if "given" is taken to mean given to a single mind which deliberately solves the problem set by these "data." It is rather a problem of how to secure the best use of resources known to any of the members of society, for ends whose relative importance only these individuals know. Or, to put it briefly, it is a problem of the utilization of knowledge which is not given to anyone in its totality'.

Given limited knowledge, competition forces market participants to make adjustment towards their own expectation. As Hayek (2002: 15) contends:

'It is precisely through the disappointment of expectations that a high degree of agreement of expectations is brought about. This fact ... is of fundamental importance in understanding the functioning of the market order. But the market's accomplishments are not exhausted in bringing about a mutual adjustment of individual plans. It also provides that every product is produced by those who can produce it more cheaply (or at least as cheaply) as anyone who does not in fact produce it, and that goods are sold at prices that are lower than those at which anyone could offer the goods who does not offer them'.

More importantly, 'competition is important only because and insofar as its outcomes are unpredictable and on the whole different from those that anyone would have been able to consciously strive for; and that its salutary effects must manifest themselves by frustrating certain intentions and disappointing certain expectations' (Hayek 2002: 10). Thus, Hayek's concept of competition is essentially a process of formation of opinion, a process which involves a continuous change in data. Hayek incorporates entrepreneurial learning, trial and error process in the market process. Moreover, he captures the essential element of competition, namely surprise and unexpected (O'Driscoll and Rizzo 1985: 102).

1.5.2 Against government intervention and central planning

Hayek argues that decentralization is the best form of economic system because of dispersed knowledge in the society. As Hayek (1949: 80) contends, 'every individual has some advantage over all others because he possesses unique information of which beneficial use might be made, but of which use can be made only if the decisions depending on it are left to him or are made with his active cooperation'. Therefore, central government cannot replace the market's ability on communicating huge amounts of complex information. On the contrary, markets allow individuals to coordinate their plans. Each market participant can almost instantaneously react to changes in market conditions. Individuals with particular knowledge of time and circumstance are far more effective in adjusting to changing economic conditions than government officials. With a dynamic market that is constantly changing, the government can never capture the information necessary to allocate resources efficiently (Brough 2002). In Hayek's words (1949: 83-84),

> 'If we can agree that the economic problem of society is mainly one of rapid adaptation to changes in the particular circumstances of time and place, it would seem to follow that the ultimate decisions must be left to the people who are familiar with these circumstances, who know directly of the relevant changes and of the resources immediately available to meet them. *We cannot expect that this problem will be solved by first communicating all this knowledge to a central board* which, after integrating all knowledge, issues its orders. We must solve it by some form of decentralization. But this answers only part of our problem. We need decentralization because only thus can we insure that the knowledge of the particular circumstances of time and place will be promptly used. But the "man on the spot" cannot decide solely on the basis of his limited but intimate knowledge of the facts of his immediate surroundings. There still remains the problem of communicating to him such further information as he needs to fit his decisions into the whole pattern of changes of the larger economic system' [italics added].

The implications of knowledge limitations on development policy can be further seen in his Nobel Memorial Lecture delivered in 1974 (Hayek 1984):

> 'If man is not to do more harm than good in his efforts to improve the social order, he will have to learn that in this, as in all other

> fields where essential complexity of an organised kind prevails, he cannot obtain the full knowledge that would make mastery of the events possible. He will therefore have to use what knowledge he can achieve, not to shape the results as the craftsman shapes his handiwork, but rather to cultivate the growth by providing the appropriate environment, in the manner which the gardener does this for his plants ... The recognition of the insuperable limits to his knowledge ought indeed to teach the student of society a lesson in humility which should guard him against becoming an accomplice in men's fatal striving to control society – a striving which makes him not only a tyrant over his fellows, but which may well make him the destroyer of a civilization which no brain has designed but which has grown from the free efforts of millions of individuals'.

Hailing Hayek, O'Driscoll (1995) concludes that the only social system ever evolved for accomplishing the task is that of private property under the rule of law. That system provides individuals with incentives to use their informational advantages, a price system to efficiently convey dispersed bits of economic information, and a legal framework for appropriating and transferring property.

1.6 Israel M. Kirzner: entrepreneurial discovery as the engine of economic growth

In dealing with economic development, Kirzner strongly criticizes mainstream neoclassical economists for their aggregation approach and neglect of entrepreneurial discovery. For Kirzner, deliberate planning is the same as discovery. Kirzner (1985: 68) states:

> 'treating the economy as a whole and abstracting from the opportunities created by interpersonal error within the system inevitably diverts analytical attention from discovery process made necessary and possible by such error. Treating growth simply as a phenomenon best achieved through deliberate planning inevitably clamps economic growth into a framework from which open-ended discovery is excluded'.

The mainstream neoclassical paradigm, in Kirzner's view, assumes that the economy is rigidly constrained by resource scarcity so that economic growth follows along certain definite path. In this context, nothing can be discovered regarding new ways of using given resources or regarding the existence of hitherto unnoticed resources. As Kirzner (1985: 70) puts it:

> '... the opportunities for growth were seen as marked out, given initial technology by a clearly defined array of inter-temporal investment possibilities that somehow existed apart from any need for them to be discovered, and whose very existence dictated the appropriate growth path. There was no suggestion that the set of opportunities likely to be in fact discovered might in some way depend on the institutional framework within which growth was sought'.

According to Kirzner (1969: 116-117), literatures on economic growth and development consist of comprehensive discussions of what possibilities exist for raising the productivity of labour, increasing the volume of resources, accumulating physical and human capital, obtaining gains through foreign trade and foreign capital. The literatures also recognise the role of technology in economic growth. However, technology only appears in an impersonal manner and can be obtained without effort by all members of the society. Entrepreneurship in these literatures is treated more or less the same way as economic resources in general. Although a difference is made between entrepreneurs and managers by contemporary neoclassical economists, the former have been treated as an element that extends the range of possible opportunities, rather than the element needed to ensure a tendency toward the fulfilment of opportunities available in principle without them.

Like Hayek, Kirzner regards economic development of a nation as a process of the interaction of millions of individual acts of mutual discovery. More precisely, Kirzner focuses on the role of entrepreneurial discovery as the engine of economic growth. For Kirzner, technical knowledge can be treated as a kind of resource but the knowledge of the availability of opportunity cannot be treated in this way. Economic development consists not only of technical knowledge but also of the exploitation of opportunities. It occurs 'not because of the availability of new opportunities, but because of expanded awareness of existing opportunities' (Kirzner 1985: 74).

Along Kirzner's line of thinking, two problems thus need to be addressed for developing economies. The first is the determination of the best course of economic development available to the society. It is a matter of comparing alternative possibilities with available resources and technology.

The second is to ensure that the opportunities thus computed will be fulfilled. No matter what form of economic organisation, whether central planning or market economy, the central issue is to ensure that existing opportunities will be discovered and seized. It is here that the entrepreneur plays a significant role (Kirzner 1969: 116). Moreover, entrepreneurial discovery will further create new information to be discovered. Hence, entrepreneurial discovery is the foundation of economic achievement in capitalism. As Kirzner (1985: 162) puts it, entrepreneurship consists of

> 'the social integration of the innumerable scraps of existing information that are present in scattered form throughout society ... Yet the same entrepreneurial spirit that stimulated the discovery of the value of information now existing throughout the market also tends to stimulate the discovery or creation of entirely new information concerning ways to anticipate or to satisfy consumer preferences. The entrepreneurial process at this second level is what drives the capitalist system toward higher and higher standards of achievement'.

Like Von Mises and Hayek, Kirzner is a defender of private property rights system and free market economy. Kirzner argues the superiority of a free society in the context of entrepreneurial discovery. For Kirzner (1979: 237-8), a free society is the one in which individuals are free to discover the available range of alternatives. Individual freedom is significant for society because it stimulates each individual to discover what opportunities confronting him/her. An environment of freedom encourages individuals to discover what opportunities each of them face. Restrictions on economic freedom harm society. They restrain the society from achieving its full potential. The restriction of economic freedom may hinder individuals from discovering opportunities they might have noticed if they had been free to exploit them. On the other hand, 'a free society is fertile and creative in the sense that its freedom generates alertness to possibilities that may be of use to society: a restriction on the freedom of society numbs each alertness and blinds society to possibilities of social improvement' (Kirzner 1979: 239). In Kirzner's view (1985: 141), government regulation discourages or hampers the discovery process. Since entrepreneurial alertness and discovery allow an individual to heap pure economic profit, it follows that 'government regulation plainly bars exploitation of opportunities for pure entrepreneurial profit. A price ceiling, a price floor, an impeded merger, or an imposed safety requirement might block possibly profitable entrepreneurial actions'.

1.7 Implications on constructing an Austrian model of economic development

We can now draw some implications on the construction of an Austrian model of economic development:

1. An Austrian theory of economic development must build on uncertainty, knowledge, error and time. As Nelson and Winter (1982: 31) notes, during economic change, there are 'diversities of viewpoint, the difficulties of the decision process, the importance of search and alertness, the value of problem-solving and errors in decisions'. Only by emphasizing on structural uncertainty and limited knowledge that we can fully understand the difficulty of human agents in making decision, or in making an innovative move.
2. Production takes on a roundabout process with goods of higher order to produce goods of lower order. Austrian economists such as Hayek, Von Mises and Lachmann always stress that capital goods are heterogeneous and complementary in nature. Hence, facing with structural uncertainty, capital combination using lengthening production process is never an easy job (Lachmann 1978; Yu 1999). Furthermore, the ultimate aim of production is to satisfy needs which are dictated by consumers. The value of production is therefore governed by consumer sovereignty in economic development.[8]
3. If economic growth means taking on roundabout production methods, then the role of entrepreneurship is to discover those alternative production opportunities. With structural uncertainty and limited knowledge, entrepreneurs attempt to put together goods of higher order to produce goods of lower order by trial and error, experimentation, learning and revisions of plans.
4. For each lengthening of the production process, entrepreneurs need to do economic calculation according to market price signals. In other words, profit and loss guide their innovative acts. Through economic calculation, errors will be eliminated, plans will be revised and capital structure will be re-shuffled. Thus, the process of economic growth is indeed a process of entrepreneurial interpretation and learning.
5. Given dispersed knowledge in the society, competition and private property rights will ensure entrepreneurial alertness and discovery, hence, economic progress. Many government interventions may hamper economic progress. In line with the Austrian thinking, perhaps

[8] Kirzner (1979: 162) refers Menger's argument that 'men value goods according to the value of the satisfactions that depends on possession of those goods' to as Menger's law.

a proper role of government in economic development is to facilitate coordination during rapid economic change (Yu 2000: 994-1013).

In conclusion, the development path of a nation is always an unintended consequence of economizing individuals and the economy will cruise towards a journey of unknown future. Austrian economics provides plentiful resources for us to formulate a useful theory of economic development.

References

Anderson, W.L. (2001) The Economics of Bad Service. *The Free Market*, vol. 19 (10), October, Mises Institute; http: //www.mises.org/freemarketdetail.aspx?Control=377; retrieved on 7 September, 2007.

Boettke, P. (2005) The Role of Private Property in a Free Society. *Virginia Viewpoint*, April no.2; http: //www.virginiainstitute.org/viewpoint/2005042.html, retrieved on 6 September 2007.

Brough, W.T. (2002) Economic Liberty and Government Growth. *Freedom Works*, February 12; http: //www.freedomworks.org/informed/issues template.php?issue_id=824, retrieved on 6 September 2007.

Gunning, P. (2009) Consumer Sovereignty: the Key to Mises's Economics. Working paper, http: //it.stlawu.edu/sdae/aelistpapers/consumer%20Sovereignty_%20the%20Key%20to%20Misess%20Economics%20rev.pdf, retrieved on 20 May 2010.

Hayek, F.A. (1949) *Individualism and Economic Order.* London, UK: Routledge and Kegan.

Hayek, F.A. (1952/1979) *The Counter Revolution of Science: Studies on the Abuse of Reason.* Indianapolis, USA: Liberty Press, pp. 141-152.

Hayek, F.A. (1968) The Defence of Our Civilization Against Intellectual Error. Reprinted in *The Freeman*, vol. 42 (6/June), 1992, The Foundation for Economic Education.

Hayek, F.A. (1984) The Pretence of Knowledge (Nobel Prize Lecture). In: C. Nishiyama and K. Leube (ed.) *The Essence of Hayek.* Stanford, USA: Hoover Institution Press, pp. 266-280.

Hayek, F.A. (2002) Competition as Discovery Process. *Quarterly Journal of Austrian Economics*, vol. 5 (3), 9-23.

Holcombe, R. (1998) Entrepreneurship and Economic Growth. *Quarterly Journal of Austrian Economics*, vol. 2 (June), 45-62.

Kirzner, I.M. (1969). Entrepreneurship and the Market Approach to Development. In: I.M. Kirzner *Perception, Opportunity and Profit.* Chicago, USA: University of Chicago Press, 1979, pp. 107-119.

Kirzner, I.M. (1979) *Perception, Opportunity and Profit: Studies in the Theory of Entrepreneurship.* Chicago, USA: University of Chicago Press.

Kirzner, I.M. (1985) *Discovery and the Capitalist Process.* Chicago, USA: University of Chicago Press.

Kirzner, I.M. (ed.) (1994) *Classics in Austrian Economics.* 3 volumes, London, UK: William Pickering and Chatto Publishers, Ltd.

Lachmann, L.M. (1978) *Capital and Its Structure.* Kansas City, USA: Sheed Andrews and Mcmeel Inc.

Littlechild, S. (ed.) (1990) *Austrian Economics.* Vol. III, Aldershot, UK: Edward Elgar.

Menger, C. (1871/1994) *Principles of Economics.* Grove City, USA: Libertarian Press.

Moss, L.S. (ed.) (1976) *The Economics of Ludwig von Mises: Toward a Critical Reappraisal.* Kansas City, USA: Sheed and Ward, Inc.

Nelson, R.R. and S.G. Winter (1982) *An Evolutionary Theory of Economic Change.* Cambridge, USA: Harvard University Press.

O'Driscoll Jr., G.P. and M. Rizzo (1985) *The Economics of Time and Ignorance.* Oxford, UK: Blackwell.

O'Driscoll Jr., G.P. (1995) The Meaning of Hayek. Cato Policy Report, November/December; http: //www.cato.org/pubs/policy_report/pr-nd-gd.html, retrieved on 7 September, 2007.

Shand, A. (1984) *The Capitalist Alternative.* Brighton, UK: Wheatsheaf Books.

Von Bohm-Bawerk, E. (1890) *Capital and Interest: A Critical History of Economical Theory,* translated by W.A. Smart. London, UK: Macmillan & Co.; http: //www.econlib.org/library/BohmBawerk/bbCI1.html, retrieved 4 September 2007.

Von Bohm-Bawerk, E. (1891) *The Positive Theory of Capital,* translated by W.A. Smart. London, UK: Macmillan & Co.; http: //www.econlib.org/ library/BohmBawerk/bbPTC8.html, retrieved 4 September 2007.

Von Mises, L. (1922/1981) *Socialism: An Economic and Sociological Analysis,* translated by J. Kahane, Foreword by F.A. Hayek. Indianapolis, USA: Liberty Fund.

Von Mises, L. (1949/1963) *Human Action,* 3rd edition. Chicago, USA: Contemporary Books Inc.

Yu, T.F-L. (1999) Toward a Praxeological Theory of the Firm. *Review of Austrian Economics,* vol. 12 (1), 25-41.

Yu, T.F-L. (2000) A New Perspective on the Role of the Government in Economic Development: Coordination under Uncertainty. *International Journal of Social Economics,* vol. 27 (7-10), 994-1013.

Chapter 2. Bringing human agency back in: a subjectivist approach to economic development

2.1 Orthodox neoclassical approaches to economic development: a critique

The orthodox neoclassical approach to economic development has long been criticized.[9] Its assumptions of rational human conduct, frictionless decision making and profit maximization distance it from reality (Schumpeter 1934/1961: 80). It 'fails to address uncertainty, bounded rationality, the presence of large corporations, institutional complexity or the dynamics of actual adjustment processes' (Nelson and Winter 1982: 5). Knowledge in the neoclassical growth modelling is treated with a sausage-machine: 'one pours inputs like capital and labor into the meat grinder of R&D and out comes knowledge, which shifts the production function' (Langlois 2010). In such approach, there is no room for enterprising and innovations, clever strategies, ingenious schemes, or charisma and more seriously; no need for mutual information among individual participants in the market process (Baumol 1968: 68; Leibenstein 1968: 72; Kirzner 1985: 16). As Hall and Rosenberg (2010: 2) rightly put it, 'an account of how and why economic change took place was precisely something that could not be provided within the "rigorously static" framework of neoclassical equilibrium analysis'. In essence, the major drawback in the mainstream neoclassical approach is that it ignores knowledge and learning.[10] The economy in this paradigm thus follows a very definite path. Accordingly, nothing can be discovered regarding new ways of using given resources or regarding the existence of hitherto unnoticed resources. Israel Kirzner (1979: 108) urges us to re-examine the role of entrepreneurship in economic development.

[9] For a review of the critiques of the orthodox neoclassical theory of economic development, see Yu (1997: 12-20).

[10] Though in recent years, the new growth theories attempt to address the knowledge problem by introducing a concept called 'knowledge filter'. However, Langlois (2010) contends that this concept is 'just another black box that can be sized to fit whichever facts (stylized or real) one has at hand'. He suggested to discard new growth models altogether and 'think hard about the structure of knowledge and how it has interacted with institutions and organizational forms'.

2.2 Uncertainty, knowledge problems and entrepreneurship as the centre of economic analysis

Challenging the neoclassical orthodoxy, the Austrian School economists place entrepreneurship at the centre of economic analysis.[11] Unlike neoclassical economics which assumes static uncertainty,[12] economic analysis in entrepreneurial perspective deals with structural uncertainty.[13] Given genuine uncertainty, entrepreneurs perceive external events, formulate plans according to their experience and knowledge. With new information and experience, they subsequently revise their plans in order to eliminate errors. As Gerald O'Driscoll and Mario Rizzo (1985: 37) note, this entrepreneurial process which involves learning is 'more than mathematical computation, rather it consists of the setting up of the problem situation itself or the movement from one problem situation to another'. It takes place when the entrepreneur's framework of interpreting external messages of stimuli has changed over time. It is imperative to understand the origin of an entrepreneurial agent's interpretation framework.

2.3 Foundations of the Austrian subjectivist approach

Cognitive studies have provided us with some profound models explaining how human agents handle problems under uncertainty. For example, Earl (1983: 140) argues that under genuine uncertainty, human agents attempt to cope with the external world by constructing, in their minds, templates of features of the world and then seeing whether these templates actually fit. Similarly, Choi (1993, 1999) argues that under uncertain environments, human agents endeavour to derive a set of usable paradigms, through a mental experimentation of their own, based on their past experiences. Likewise, Lane *et al.* (1996: 53) argue that, when confronted with a new situation requiring action, our mental system,

---

[11] For recent examples of this kind of study, see Foss *et al.* (2008) and High (2009).

[12] According to Arrow (1974: 33), uncertainty in the conventional neoclassical sense refers to the situation 'that we do not have a complete description of the world which we fully believe to be true. Instead, we consider the world to be in one or another of a range of states. Each state of the world is a description which is complete for all relevant purposes'. This sort of uncertainty consists in not knowing which state is the true one.

[13] Structural uncertainty refers not only to the situation in which people do not know the chances of various outcomes, but in which they do not know what outcomes are possible. They may well be far from sure even of the structures of the problem that they encounter.

> 'categorises the situation according to patterns motivated by previously experienced situations. The categories are associated with particular actions: the association depends upon the valuations of the effects of the actions taken in past situations that were characterised similarly to the present situation. The categorisation-action system then generates an action on the basis of this association'.

While cognitive studies focus on agents' reaction to the external environment, the Austrian subjectivist approach is more deeply rooted in the Schutzian theory of human agency and emphasizes the point that a human agent's stock of knowledge has a particular history. It has been constituted in and by previous experience activities of an agent's consciousness (Schutz 1970: 74; Berger and Berger 1976). Though this stock of knowledge, accumulated from experiences, can be modified over time; it cannot be 'sought' or 'searched' for as a paradigm, as argued by Choi (1993).

2.4 Human action, sense-making and the formation of interpretation framework

Human agents act in everyday life. They act on the basis of thinking (Knight, 1956: 123). Each action has a meaning attached to it. Actors do not live alone but experience with the existence of other people. In other words, they make sense of the social world (Weick 1969). Sense-making implies interpretation. Actors try to understand other people and expect other people to understand them (Weber 1964; Goffman 1969). In simple terms, action is intersubjective. Individuals find themselves related to the surrounding world in order to create a meaningful life and share it with others. In other words, it is only in the common-sense world that we can communicate and formulate plans.

People act, experience and learn from their everyday lives. Their experiences accumulate into a stock of knowledge for them to interpret the outside world. Human agents find, at any given point of time, a stock of knowledge at hand that serves them as a scheme of interpretation of their past and present experiences, and determines their anticipation of things to come (Schutz 1970: 74). When we experience, our knowledge grows.[14] Experiences enter the individual's consciousness via everyday life

[14] For an exposition concerning entrepreneurial learning and the growth of knowledge from the Popperian perspective, see Harper (1996).

learning, such as daily contact with our parents, face-to-face interaction with friends and our neighbourhood, watching television and movies and so on. This means that the framework is largely biographically determined (Berger and Berger 1976). These lived experiences are then typified and crystallized into routines or rules of thumb which can be used as a skill or problem-solving technique in everyday life. As soon as we encounter an event, we can follow the established interpretative channel and have access to all knowledge (meaning) about that event (DeBono 1980: 14). It is like steering a car. When we are on a familiar road, we do not need to use a map or read road signs for directions. Similarly, our interpretation frameworks continue to search for familiar roads that render thinking unnecessary. Furthermore, unlike the environmental or behavioural school which emphasizes the agents' adaptive response to external factors, scholars in the action frame of reference believe that human agents 'enact' with rather than 'react' to their environment (Weick 1969: 27; Jehenson 1973: 235; Jones 1987: 24). In this framework, human action is not seen as a given response to some external stimuli, but arises out of the meaning and significance people construct in events. Bringing to bear personal frameworks of beliefs and values that actors have developed over their lives, they subjectively and selectively define situations (Jones 1987: 24). As Weick (1969: 27) argues, 'instead of adapting to a ready-made environment ... actors themselves create the environment to which they adapt'. Shackle (1958: 21) takes a radical subjectivist view and argues that the entrepreneur can 'create imagined results'. By acting differently, he or she can make a difference (White 1977: 67). In other words, human agents define their future and their reality (Berger and Luckmann 1966). Hence, the stock of knowledge that actors possess is by no means homogeneous (Schutz 1970: 74). Because of diverse experiences, human agents will respond differently to the same objectively defined stimulus[15] (O'Driscoll and Rizzo 1985: 38-39; Yu 1999). In Lachmann's words (1970: 36), 'different men in identical situations may act differently because of their different expectations of the future'. Interpretations provide the basis for expectations concerning the other's next move. Hence, expectations are more than prediction or

[15] Simmel (1918/1980: 57-92) identifies two modes of understanding, namely, historical and immanent. On the one hand, an interpretation may represent an answer to a question about the conditions for the production of the interpretandum. In that case, the question is historical and the interpretans produces a historical interpretation. On the other hand, the interpretation may represent an answer to a question about the intrinsic properties of the interpretation itself. A description of these properties is independent of any description of the genesis of the interpretandum. The question is then immanent. The argument that human agents will respond differently to the same objectively-defined stimulus belongs to the former, that is, the historical question.

anticipation; they are social realities. In conclusion, the interpretation framework developed in our mind allows us to make sense of the world and to solve problems. Without such a system, coordination of economic activities would be impossible.

The interpretation framework, originating from the actor's lived experiences, is a device for receiving external information and organizes itself into patterns. Once the patterns are formed, the framework will be used as a broad catchment area for interpreting incoming events which involves a sorting of new experiences into existing categories, sometimes adding to or modifying the structure as a result. The framework helps an individual to identify and solve problems, and discover opportunities. However, the patterns are not symmetric. The lack of symmetry gives rise to new ideas and creativity (DeBono 1992: 15).

2.5 Entrepreneurial learning and the market process

Entrepreneurial discovery is a learning process. Human agents are not passive receptors of information. They learn selectively and engage in the ordering and selection of information pertinent to their particular situation and objectives. Knowledge and history shape agents' interpretation of their environments, hence, their discoveries and institutions. Gifford's concept of limited entrepreneurial attention (1992: 276-278) postulates that, facing complexity in everyday life and the possibility of the projection of many imagined worlds, entrepreneurs tend to expose themselves to ideas that are in accordance with their interests, needs, or existing attitudes. They consciously or unconsciously avoid messages that are in conflict with their predispositions. Rogers (1983: 166) calls this 'selective exposure'. In Schutz's terms (1970: 111-112), agents' prevailing systems of interests or 'systems of relevance' determine the elements of their stock of knowledge. The particular system of relevance guides the entrepreneur and influences the sort of discoveries he or she can make. As Hayek (1952: 139) puts it, attention 'is thus always directed, or confined to a particular class of events for which we are on the look-out and which, in consequence, we perceive with greater distinctness when one of them occurs'.

2.6 Trial and error elimination

Entrepreneurs learn by trial and error, a measure adopted by most organisms. Karl Popper (1972: 242) argues 'all organisms are constantly ... engaging in problem solving' which 'always proceeds by the method of trial and error; new reactions, new forms, new organs, new modes of behavior, new hypothesis, are tentatively put forward and controlled by error-elimination.' Agreeing with Popper, F.A. Hayek argues that discovery is an evolutionary process of cumulative growth of problem-solving knowledge. In Hayek's view, the market is an ongoing, open-ended process of trial-and-error elimination, a process in which a number of potential alternative solutions of various kinds of problems are constantly tried out and selected through the choices of market participants. It is a process in which new tentative problem-solutions are continuously explored, and in which the problems themselves are subject to change, as solutions to old problems tend to create new problems. The learning or discovery process involves the history of the entrepreneur's own experience of success and failure. Agents interpret or classify incoming events according to their own experience. Whenever the expectations resulting from the existing interpretation are disappointed, or when beliefs so far held are disproved by new experience, then re-interpretation or reclassification occurs. The whole process of entrepreneurial learning, of the growth of knowledge, is then seen as consisting of such re-interpretation or reclassification, as a process in which our 'frame of reference' is corrected, adjusted, or refined (Vanberg 1994: 97).

2.7 Competition, market selection and coordination

Entrepreneurs' subjective interpretation of incoming events and the choice of an option are subject to market tests. Market selection in economics consists of three parts: variation, selection, and retention. Variation occurs through entrepreneurship. Selection will typically occur through the realization of profit and loss. In the filtering process, those options yielding profits will be selected while those options leading to losses will be eliminated. Profitability governs the market selection. Once new ways of doing things are found profitable or feasible, business people will use them repeatedly. In other words, these rules are adopted (retention). Hayek argues that the limits of our reason require us to follow rules. Rules are the device for coping with our ignorance (Hayek 1960: 66, 1967: 90, 1976: 8). The whole rationale of the phenomenon of rule-guided action is to be found in our inescapable ignorance of most of the particular circumstances which determine the effects of our actions (Hayek 1967: 90). Rules facilitate the making of decisions in complex situations. They limit our range of choice by reducing the list of circumstances which we need to take into account in particular circumstances, singling out certain classes of facts as alone determining the general kind of action which we should take (Hayek 1964: 11; Vanberg 1993: 182).

Entrepreneurs are constantly engaged in solving novel problems (Harper 1994: 56). What is learned may be 'false' and entrepreneurs may fail. The market system is not a system of profit and profit; it is a system of profit and loss. Whenever actual events diverge from predictions, entrepreneurs learn that something is wrong with their stock of knowledge. They know that they cannot hold on to their existing conjectural framework (*ibid.*: 63). Simply put, the failure of a plan must be due to inadequate knowledge of the circumstances in which the action has to be taken. Previously unsuccessful plans prompt the need for a revision of plans. A new array of plans is formed, each with a tentative solution to the original problem. The number or variety of solutions proposed is limited by the entrepreneur's creativity and imagination. The new plan is problematic too. Each trial solution is controlled by a process of attempted error elimination. Error elimination is done through the testing of ideas in practice, which involves the comparison and assessment of rival conjectures in terms of how well they can solve the problems (*ibid.*: 72). Successful plans are adopted and imitated in the market. Reinforced by rule following, new institutions gradually emerge as social coordinators. Institutions are the resultant of millions of entrepreneurs' selective learning processes and market selections.

In summary, this chapter has acknowledged the shortcomings of the mainstream neoclassical economics in analysing development issues. It has proposed adopting an Austrian subjectivist approach to handle economic and development issues. Utilizing largely the contributions of Alfred Schutz and Austrian economists, this chapter has formulated a subjective interpretation framework originating from German and Austrian economics. Highlighting the nature of intersubjectivity in human understanding, this framework forms a base for explaining economic coordination and hence a foundation for development policies. This proposed alternative framework, which is deeply rooted in human agency, will be shown to be able to shed new light on various areas of economic development, namely, entrepreneurship, national capabilities, government, trade, innovation, transition and catching up strategies for small businesses in latecomer economies.

References

Arrow, K.J. (1974) *The Limits of Organization.* New York, USA: Norton.

Berger, P. and B. Berger (1976) *Sociology: A Biographical Approach,* revised edition. Middlesex, UK: Penguin.

Berger, P. and T. Luckmann (1966) *The Social Construction of Reality.* New York, USA: Anchor Books.

Baumol, W.J. (1968) Entrepreneurship in Economic Theory. *American Economic Review Papers and Proceedings,* vol. 58, 64-71.

Choi, Y.B. (1993) *Paradigms and Conventions: Uncertainty, Decision Making and Entrepreneurship.* Ann Arbor, USA: University of Michigan Press.

Choi, Y.B. (1999) Conventions and Economic Change: A Contribution Toward a Theory of Political Economy. *Constitutional Policy Economy,* vol. 10 (3), 245-264.

DeBono, E. (1980) *Opportunities.* Middlesex, UK: Penguin.

DeBono, E. (1992) *Serious Creativity.* New York, USA: Harper Business.

Earl, P.E. (1983) *The Economic Imagination: Towards a Behavourial Analysis of Choice.* New York, USA: Sharpe Inc.

Foss, N., P.G. Klein, Y.Y. Kor and J.T. Mahoney (2008) Entrepreneurship, Subjectivism and The Resource-Based View: Toward a New Synthesis. *Strategic Entrepreneurship Journal,* vol. 2, 73-94.

Gifford, S. (1992) Allocation of Entrepreneurial Attention. *Journal of Economic Behavior and Organization,* vol. 19, 265-283.

Goffman, E. (1969). *The Presentation Of Self In Everyday Life.* Garden City, NY, USA: Doubleday.

Hall, B.H. and N. Rosenberg (2010) *Handbook of the Economics of Innovation.* New York, USA: Elsevier.

Harper, D.A. (1994) A New Approach to Modelling Endogenous Learning Processes in Economic Theory. In: P. Boettke, I. Kirzner and M. Rizzo (eds.) *Advances in Austrian Economics I.* Greenwich, USA: JAI Press, pp. 49-79.

Harper, D.A. (1996) *Entrepreneurship and the Market Process: An Enquiry into the Growth of Knowledge.* London, UK: Routledge.

Hayek, F.A. (1952) *The Sensory Order.* Chicago, USA: University of Chicago Press.

Hayek, F.A. (1960) *The Constitution of Liberty.* Chicago, USA: University of Chicago Press.

Hayek, F.A. (1964) Kind of Order in Society. *New Individualist Review,* vol. 3 (3), 3-12.

Hayek, F.A. (1967) *Studies in Philosophy, Politics and Economics.* Chicago, USA: University of Chicago Press.

Hayek, F.A. (1976) *Law, Legislation and Liberty, Volume 2 (The Mirage of Social Justice).* London, UK: Routledge & Kegan Paul.

High, J. (2009) Entrepreneurship and Economic Growth: The Theory of Emergent Institutions. *The Quarterly Journal of Austrian Economics,* vol. 12 (3), 3-36.

Jehenson, R. (1973) A Phenomenological Approach to the Study of the Formal Organisation. In: G. Psathas (ed.), *Phenomenological Sociology Issues and Applications.* New York, USA: John Wiley, pp. 219-247.

Jones, S. (1987) Choosing Action Research: A Rationale. In: I.L. Mangham (ed.) *Organisation Analysis and Development.* New York, USA: John Wiley, pp. 234-254.

Knight, F.H. (1956) *On the History and Methods of Economics.* Chicago, USA: University of Chicago Press.

Kirzner, I.M. (1985) *Discovery and the Capitalist Process.* Chicago, USA: University of Chicago Press.

Kirzner, I.M. (1979) *Perception, Opportunity and Profit.* Chicago, USA: University of Chicago Press.

Lachmann, L.M. (1970) *The Legacy of Max Weber.* London, UK: Heinemann.

Lane, D., F. Malerba, R. Maxfield and L. Orsenigo (1996) Choice and Action. *Journal of Evolutionary Economics,* vol. 6, 43-76.

Langlois, R. (2010) The 'Knowledge Filter' and the New Economy. Organizations and Markets Blog; http: //organizationsandmarkets.com/, retrieved on 29 May 2010.

Leibenstein, H. (1968) Entrepreneurship and Development. *American Economic Review,* vol. 58, 72-83.

Nelson, R.R. and S.G. Winter (1982) *An Evolutionary Theory of Economic Change.* Cambridge, USA: Harvard University Press.

O'Driscoll, G. and M.J. Rizzo (1985) *The Economics of Time and Ignorance.* London, UK: Blackwell.

Popper, K. (1972) *Objective Knowledge: An Evolutionary Approach.* Oxford, UK: Oxford University Press.

Rogers, E.M. (1983) *Diffusion of Innovations,* 3rd. edition. New York, USA: The Free Press.

Schumpeter, J.A. (1934/1961) *The Theory of Economic Development.* New York, USA: Oxford University Press.

Schutz, A. (1970) *On Phenomenology and Social Relations.* Chicago, USA: The University of Chicago Press.

Shackle, G.L.S. (1958) *Time in Economics.* Connecticut, USA: Greenwood Press.

Simmel, G. (1918/1980) *Essays on Interpretation in Social Science.* Manchester, UK: Manchester University Press.

Vanberg, J.V. (1994) *Rules and Choice in Economics.* London, UK: Routledge.

Weber, M. (1964) *The Theory Of Social And Economic Oganisation.* New York, USA: The Free Press.

Weick, K. (1969) *The Social Psychology of Organising.* Reading, USA: Addison-Wesley.

Weick, K. (1995) *Sensemaking in Organisations.* Thousand Oaks, USA: Sage.

White, L.H. (1977) Uncertainty and Entrepreneurial Expectation in Economic Theory. Unpublished Senior Honours Thesis, Harvard College, USA, 31 March.

Yu, T.F-L. (1997) *Entrepreneurship and Economic Development in Hong Kong.* London, UK: Routledge.

Yu, T.F-L. (1999) Toward a Praxeological Theory of the Firm. *Review of Austrian Economics,* vol. 12 (1), 25-41.

Chapter 3.
The entrepreneurial process

3.1 Introduction

It is generally known that entrepreneurship has no role in contemporary mainstream neoclassical economics. The entrepreneur disappears completely in the neoclassical analysis where optimization technique and production functions are adopted. The entrepreneurial process in the neoclassical paradigm is simply a mechanic movement from disequilibrium to equilibrium through information searching. Learning in neoclassical economics is a static process involving known options (Boland 1982: 161-163).

The entrepreneurial process has been discussed and taught in management discipline. For example, Hisrich, Peters and Shepherd (2005) argue that the entrepreneurial process involves: (1) identification and evaluation of the opportunity, (2) development of the business plan, (3) determination of the required resources, and (4) management of the resulting enterprise. Many management studies also provide us with case studies to illustrate how business errors should be handled (for example, see Farson and Keyes 2002). However, in most management literatures, the analysis of the entrepreneurial process has not been centred on the theory of human agency in association with uncertainty.

Chen, Tsai and Lin (2006: 46) rightly point out that 'studies mostly focus on the successful entrepreneurs, analysing from personality or business operation performance perspectives on how they could succeed, or they often focus on how entrepreneurs avoid failures. Few studies draw their attention to the processes and progress how entrepreneurs bounce back after failures'. Hence, the entrepreneurial process deserves to be examined in detail.

Minniti and Bygrave (2001: 5-16) present a dynamic model of entrepreneurial learning which is most relevant to my work here. They argue that 'entrepreneurs learn by updating a subjective stock of knowledge accumulated on the basis of past experience'. In their view, entrepreneurs repeat only those choices that appear most promising and discard the ones that result in failure. Minniti and Bygrave's paper highlights the role of 'failure' in the information processing and concludes that 'entrepreneurs process information, make mistakes, update their decisional algorthms' and improve their performance during the struggling process.

Despite the above contributions, a satisfactory model on the entrepreneurial process in the human agency perspective is still lacking. This chapter utilises the contributions of Max Weber and Alfred Schutz, in particular their theories of human action, to understand the entrepreneurial process. Unlike Minniti and Bygrave's model which presents a mathematical model on learning in the entrepreneurial process, this chapter focuses on how the entrepreneur formulates and revises plans under uncertainty as well as learning from experience. This work differs from other entrepreneurship studies in the approach. The analysis in this chapter is deeply rooted in the phenomenological theory of human action originated in German and Austrian social sciences.

3.2 Theories of the entrepreneurial process in economics

Though contemporary mainstream economists ignore the entrepreneurial process, it is possible to churn out some ideas of the entrepreneurial process from the seminal works of Joseph Schumpeter, Israel Kirzner and Frank Knight.

3.2.1 The entrepreneurial process as a process of creative destruction: Schumpeter's contribution

According to Schumpeter (1934: 81-86), the entrepreneurial process is a process in which the entrepreneur exerts a 'creative destruction' to the traditional economy by introducing a new method of production, the opening of a new market, the utilisation of new source of raw material or intermediate good and carrying out of new organisation of an industry (Schumpeter 1934: 66). Furthermore, Schumpeter recognises that entrepreneurial innovation is a difficult job because it lies outside the routine framework. As a result, a new way of doing things encounters strong social resistance. Therefore, the entrepreneurial function does not merely invent nor create the conditions which the enterprise exploits. It consists of 'getting [new] things done' (Schumpeter 1943: 93).

The entrepreneurial process consists of two kinds of events, namely 'adaptive response' and 'creative response' (Schumpeter 1947: 150):

> 'Whenever an economy reacts to an increase in population by simply adding the new brains and hands to the working force in the existing employment, or an industry reacts to a protective duty by expansion within its existing practice, we may speak of the development as adaptive response. And whenever the economy or an industry or some firms in an industry do something else, something that is outside of the range of existing practice, we may speak of creative response'.

Moreover, adaptive response follows creative response (Schumpeter 1934/1961: 228).[16] Once the new possibility is tried, imitators who perceive the advantages of the new method will take a share in those advantages. These imitators are people who do not have the will to overcome social resistance to innovation themselves. However, they are ready to adopt new method promptly as soon as the pioneer has overcome the initial resistance. It is in this way that an innovation achieves widespread adoption in the system (Cauthorn 1989: 14). In general, Schumpeter's entrepreneurial process can be viewed as a process of technological advance.

3.2.2 The entrepreneurial process as a process of discovery and arbitrageurship: Kirzner's contribution

Kirzner's view of the entrepreneurial process departs sharply from Schumpeter. While Schumpeter views the entrepreneurial process as a process of 'creative destruction', Kirzner views it as a process of entrepreneurial alertness, discovery and opportunity exploitation. Building upon Von Mises' insight, Kirzner (1973: 33) argues that human agents attempt to remove uneasiness and make themselves better off during the entrepreneurial process. Human agents are 'endowed not only with the propensity to pursue goals efficiently, once ends and means are clearly identified, but also with the drive and alertness needed to identify which ends to strive for and which means are available'. In the market

[16] Schumpeter (1934/1961: 228) summarizes the relationship between two responses as follows: 'If one or a few have advanced with success many of the difficulties disappear. Others can then follow these pioneers, as they will clearly do under the stimulus of the success now attainable. Their success again makes it easier, through the increasingly complete removal of the obstacles ... for more people to follow suit, until finally the innovation becomes familiar and the acceptance of it a matter of free choice'.

process, entrepreneurship performs arbitrageurship function. Whenever there are mismatched markets, entrepreneurs will exploit the situation where price discrepancies occur. Kirzner (1973) argues that the existence of disequilibrium situations in the market implies profit opportunities. During the entrepreneurial process, profit opportunities are exploited, errors are eliminated, and the economy moves towards equilibrium.

3.2.3 Knight on the entrepreneurial process: uncertainty and judgement

In Knight's works, uncertainty plays a significant role in the entrepreneurial process. Facing uncertainty, the entrepreneur exercises his/her judgement (Knight 1921: 211). For Knight, entrepreneurs 'infer' largely from their experiences of the past, somewhat in the same way as we deal with simple problems such as estimating distances, weights or physical magnitudes when measuring instruments are not available. Furthermore, entrepreneurs bet on their judgements (Knight 1921: 210). Entrepreneurs try to determine what kinds of workers to be hired, what orders to be given, which non-human factors to be utilized, and how their employees will be used. They also predict future demand conditions which are partly depended upon the actions of competitors. Having made their determinations and predictions, entrepreneurs proceed to make judgements concerning the profitability of alternative actions. When they ultimately decide to hire factors and produce a product for sale, they are in effect betting that their judgements on the value of the factors they employ are more accurate than the judgements of others who are unwilling to bid as high as them. In this way, the factors of production come to be controlled and allocated by those who have the most faith and trust in their judgements (Knight, 1921: 268). However, estimates or judgements are liable to err (Knight 1921: 203, 230). Hence, profit arises from error or imperfect foresight made by the entrepreneur (Knight 1956: 24). The level of profit is not stipulated in any agreement nor fixed in an exchange but is contingent upon the success of an enterprise or undertaking.

3.3 The entrepreneurial process as a process of subjective interpretation

This chapter will present a model of the entrepreneurial process based largely on the contributions of Max Weber and Alfred Schutz and Austrian economists such as Ludwig von Mises, F.A. Hayek and Ludwig Lachmann.

As argued in Chapter 2, human action has meaning attached to it as human agents make sense out of their everyday business life (Weick 1969, 1995). Making sense of the external world means interpretation. Economic coordination involves an understanding of actions and interpretation of the meaning of other market participants. As Weigert (1981: 74) puts it, 'interpretation is a process of perceiving the other and his or her interaction within symbolic frameworks so that we can make some sense out of what the other is doing.... If we cannot make any sense out of the other's interaction, it may be that there is no sense in it, or worse, it may be that there is no sense in me'.

Experiences from everyday life are accumulated into a stock of knowledge that can be used to interpret incoming events. This stock of knowledge serves as a scheme of interpretation and determines human agent's anticipation of things to come (Schutz 1970: 74). When we experience, our knowledge grows. Experiences enter individual's consciousness via learning in everyday life, such as daily contact with parents, face-to-face interaction with friends and neighbourhood, watching television and movies and so on. Hence, the framework has a history (Berger and Berger 1976). These lived experiences are then typified and crystallized into routines or rules of thumb which can be used as a skill or problem-solving technique in everyday life. Interpretations provide the basis for expectations concerning the other person's next move. Thus, expectations are more than prediction or anticipation; they are social realities. In short, the interpretation framework developed in our mind allows us to make sense out of the world and to solve economic problems. Without such a framework, expectation and plan would be impossible.

3.3.1 Repeated incoming events and routine response

The interpretation framework, originating from the actor's lived experiences, is a device of receiving external information and organizing itself into patterns. Once patterns are formed, the framework will be used as a broad catchment area for interpreting incoming events which involve sorting new experiences into existing categories, sometimes adding to or modifying the structure as a result. The framework helps an individual to identify and solve problems, and discovers opportunities (DeBono 1992: 15). As soon as we spot something, we can follow the established interpretative channel and have access to all knowledge (meaning) about that thing (DeBono 1980: 14). In other words, if incoming events are *repeated and familiar*, the entrepreneur can utilize rules of thumbs to solve the problems. Events are thus anticipated and entrepreneur's expectation is consistent with the market participants' expectations. Economic activities are coordinated. The entrepreneur can earn profits using the same stock of knowledge to solve familiar problems.

3.3.2 Novel incoming events

What will happen if the incoming event is novel? A novel event will create new impulses to the perception process. New impulses will not be acted upon immediately in a stimulus-response manner. Instead, they will be assessed by the mind to see how these new events fit into the overall picture of the entrepreneur's mind. The selection of an appropriate response involves not only responding to one impulse with one action, but also drawing upon a record of associations in the past (Fleetwood 1995: 115). Some completely new pattern of events can be classified, not because it is governed by a particular rule that still exists. Rather, it is because the pattern is similar to some previously observed patterns in which an abstract, general rule of action has already existed.

Entrepreneurs are able to perceive and classify actions that they may have never seen before, and thereby initiate an appropriate action in response because they have an internalized stock of similar general rules. A mechanism of sensory pattern transfer is in operation. In other words, patterns learned in one format can be transferred to another so that a pattern is recognised in a different format. Without the capacity to transfer patterns across the fields, entrepreneurs would be incapable of understanding any kind of novel behaviour (Fleetwood 1995: 112).

However, if the event is truly novel, the established linkages of the mental map often fail to give an adequate account of the new environment in which entrepreneurs find themselves. Neither can they give a correct projection of the immediate future (i.e. they make a wrong prediction). In other words, the stock of existing rules is inapplicable to the new event. If this is the case, then the entrepreneur is in a state of conflicting experience, two results may occur. The entrepreneur either continues to use old methods to solve new problems or devises new methods to tackle new problems.

3.3.2.1 Using old methods to tackle new problems

Perceiving novel events, some agents may continue to use old methods to solve new problems. This response does not catch up with the changing market condition and is doomed to fail. A reason why business people refuse to change is inertia. Resistance to change is fundamentally associated with mental thinking. As mentioned, the agent's stock of knowledge is a product of subjective interpretation, reclassification and learning. Agents' interpretation process has certain time sequence that allows thinking to follow a routine perception track. In other words, agents see things in a certain way and expect things to be worked out in a certain way. Once the incoming information is organized into a (mental) pattern, then the agents' subjective interpretation framework no longer has to categorize incoming information. All that is required is to have enough information to trigger the pattern. The mind then follows along the pattern automatically in the same way as a driver follows a familiar road. Over time, a habit develops because the actor simply uses his or her interpretation system routinely. Resistance to change means that actors' thinking is locked up in the old interpretation structure or concepts (DeBono 1992: 17). Two further points are worth to mention. Firstly, once agents take the stock of knowledge for granted, then perception becomes even more influential, because the way they look at a situation will determine what they can do about it. Secondly, unless another competing pattern is developed in the agent's interpretation framework, anything similar to the established pattern will be treated just as if it were that pattern. It is just like a watershed. Unless there is a competing tributary, water will gather into the main stream flowing downhill. Furthermore, the stock of knowledge is also a product of social construction. Rules or moral norms are then followed unconditionally for agents always consider their actions as 'right'. If they act against these rules, then they will have a 'bad conscience'. Hence, an action is reinforced during the process of socialization when agents learn to behave according to the 'right' rules of the game that constitute the society they live in (Ackermann 1998).

It may be argued that whenever interpreting incoming events is necessary, actors should not take their experience or knowledge for granted. Unfortunately, as Allen and Haas (2001: 25) note, all psychological changes are very hard to bring about. It is often the case that individuals are unwilling to let go of existing concepts or perceptions in order to put both previous and recent experiences into a new perspective.[17] As explained above, rule-following has its merits. After a period of time, as the pattern in agents' minds survives for too long, it will become non-separable and resist disruption. In other words, over time each piece of knowledge works

[17] In a cognitive study, Wu *et al.* (2009) tried to explain the entrepreneurs' mental modification process and coping strategies when facing the failure.

together, forming an integrated part of cognitive pattern, and is reinforced by social norms, customs and routines. By that time, changing patterns will become extremely difficult (DeBono 1992: 17).

3.3.2.2 Devising new methods to tackle new problems: adaptive learning

Most entrepreneurs will devise new methods if they find that prevailing methods are unable to solve new problems. They learn to adopt new methods by trial and error and experimentation. Encountering uncertainty, they will cope with their knowledge-deficiency by creating temporary expectations which serve as knowledge surrogates (White 1977: 80). Schutz (1970) refers to this as projected action in the future perfect tense (see also Weick 1969). In other words, the entrepreneur will project and plan as if it were a complete act. This knowledge surrogate will be experimented in the market. If this works, then the method will be adopted and routinized as a rule of thumb. The new stock of knowledge the entrepreneur possessed can once again serve as an interpretative framework which enables him or her to anticipate things to come and thus coordinate economic activities. Correctly anticipating things to come or correct interpretation will bring business profit to the entrepreneur. Minniti and Bygrave (2001: 5) rightly remark that entrepreneurial decisions are 'the result of an entrepreneur's ability to process information (knowledge), and of random impulses (instinct or luck). In the long run, it is the knowledge component that determines the entrepreneur's selection of the most appropriate course of action in any specific uncertain environment. In particular, ... entrepreneurs learn from successes as well as failures'.

3.3.3 Entrepreneurship and creating uncertainty

If joy repeatedly occurs, human agents will find everyday life less exciting. Boring can be even more devastating than the pain of failures (Farson and Keyes 2002: 47). This explains why many people give up a steady and well-paid job and attempt new adventures. Human agents want to shield themselves off from uncertainty. Paradoxically, they also create uncertainty for themselves by venturing into some unknown businesses. Entrepreneurs long for the reward behind uncertain investment but they do not necessarily enjoy the reward afterwards. Atari's founder, Nolan Bushnell, once said: 'landing the success is boring' (Farson and Keyes 2002: 47). Creating uncertainty and learning to solve problems from failures is to overtake oneself.[18] Hence, people do not necessarily reject change or crisis. On the other hand, receiving challenge makes us grow. Entrepreneurs often enjoy the process more than the harvest. Facing challenge, they energize their minds to solve problems.

The theory of human agency argues that we are not passive robots. We do not only adapt ourselves to the external world but also adjust the environment to our needs through deliberate and conscious choices. Besides being diffusers and users of knowledge, human agents are also the source of knowledge. In other words, they are the builders and users of knowledge, creators of economic processes and above all, the engines of change (Hayek 1952; see also Rizzello 2000). In this regard, economic change is connected with the fact that human agents constantly create the reasons for their own existence, attempt to influence as much as possible and thus determine the future states of the world in a direction that favours their own development (Rizzello 2000: 127-150). This is the foundation of entrepreneurial discoveries.

Furthermore, unlike the environmental or behavioural school which emphasizes the agents' adaptive response to external factors, scholars in the action frame of reference believe that human agents 'enact' with rather than 'react' to their environment (Weick 1969: 27; Jones 1987: 24). In this framework, human action is not seen as a given response to some external stimuli, but arises out of the meaning and significance people construct in events. Bringing to bear personal frameworks of beliefs and values that actors have developed over their lives, they subjectively and selectively define situations (Jones 1987: 24). As Weick (1969: 27) argues, 'instead of adapting to a ready-made environment ... actors themselves create the environment to which they adapt'. Shackle (1958: 21) takes a radical subjectivist view and argues that the entrepreneur can 'create imagined results'. By acting differently, human agents can make a difference to the external world (White 1977: 67). In other words, they define their future and their reality (Berger and Luckmann 1966). In the Schutzian perspective, the process of entrepreneurial innovation can be roughly classified into four stages.

[18] French politician, Georges Clemenceau once notes, 'failure means one tries to overtake oneself' (Farson and Keyes 2002: 71).

3.3.3.1 Projection, focus, elaboration and implementation

1. Projecting a profit opportunity: fantasy and imagination
Entrepreneurial innovation is essentially a mental projection, involving initially some fantasies. Fantasy refers to the world-building capability of human imagination (Weigert 1981: 138-141). Fantasy can range from a carefully prepared plan, through a detailed imagined scenario to an unrealistic sheer fantasy. 'Realistic' fantasy is the plan. During the infant stage of mental projection (Schutz 1970: 125-159), entrepreneurs envisage a new product or a new method of production in their mind (Vesper 1990: 98). At this point, actors are not impeded by any limits imposed by reality. They simply mentally apply new ideas to their anticipated future before deciding to try it or not (Rogers 1983: 170). The ability to think hypothetically and counter factually and to project it to the future is an important mental capacity of the entrepreneur in the market process. Entrepreneurs fantasise something that has not yet occurred or may never occur (Schutz 1970: 125-159; Weigert 1981: 139). However, the contents of fantasy are shaped by entrepreneurs' experiences or stocks of knowledge.

2. Focus of an idea: the entrepreneurial selective attention
Facing complexity in everyday life and the possibility of the projection of many imagined worlds, how can the actor handle the situation and come up with a selected plan? In a cognitive study, March and Simon (1958) highlight the entrepreneurial attention by classifying actions which maintain going concerns and those by devising and evaluating new programs. Along this line of thinking, Gifford (1992: 276-278) proposes a concept of limited entrepreneurial attention. She postulates that the entrepreneur will allocate his/her attention between current operations and prospective new projects, depending on the relative profit between two projects. In phenomenology, the entrepreneurial attention depends on relevance.[19] Schutz and Luckmann (1989: 32) argue that the actor does not consider many future possibilities at once. Individuals tend to expose themselves to ideas in accordance with their interests, needs, or existing

[19] As suggested by Schutz (1970: 111-112), there are four zones of relevance with respect to entrepreneurial interest, each of them requiring different degree of knowledge. The four zones are: (a) Primary relevance – the part of the world within our reach which can be at once observed by us and also partially controlled by the actor. This region can be materialised by the agents and requires the knowledge of know-how. (b) Related primary relevance – the part of the world that is not open to our domination but provides us with ready-made tool for attaining goals. (c) Relatively irrelevance – the part of the world that has no connection with the actor's interests at hand. (d) Absolutely irrelevance – no possible change occurring within them would influence the target of the agents.

attitudes. They consciously or unconsciously avoid messages that are in conflict with their predispositions. This idea is similar to Rogers' (1983: 166) concept of selective exposure. Entrepreneurs will expose themselves to an opportunity which is relevant to their needs, interests and consistent with their existing attitudes and beliefs. The interest at hand determines the system of relevance. The relevance zone is neither constant nor homogeneous because human agents have disparate interests (Weigert 1981: 61).

3. Elaboration of an opportunity
'To get the things done', the entrepreneur implements production plans (Schumpeter 1934: 86-87; Rogers 1983: 174). Thus, the entrepreneur attempts to 'invent the future in a profitable image, an image as agreeable as possible to the future customers' (White 1977: 71). However, to transform imagination into reality, entrepreneurs encounter 'practicabilities problems' (Schutz and Luckmann 1989). According to Schutz, practicabilities are related to two interconnected presuppositions for the realisation of a project. First, actors estimate the objective conditions for reaching their goals and second, actors estimate their capacities to carry out the performance of the acts. For an opportunity to be practical, actors think that they can transform what they project into reality. This bases on the assumption that today is essentially the same as yesterday and tomorrow will be like today. Hence, actors assume that they can do things today and tomorrow as what they did yesterday. In Husseslian categories: 'I can always do it again and so forth' which has a biographical dimension (Schutz and Luckmann 1989: 25-26). The estimation of practicability of a certain project assumes 'the continued existence of the world as I know it and of my continued existence in it as I know myself.' Upon this, actors apply the knowledge of the type of objects and events. Of this, habitual knowledge is important where functions consist mainly of simplifying everyday life, e.g. skill is a habitual function of bodily movement. On the other hand, specific knowledge is project-relevant: knowledge limits an individual's reach and capacity to operate (Schutz and Luckmann 1989: 26).

4. Implementing a project
Actors imaginatively run through a series of psychic states and they must decide which particular future to be wanted by themselves (Schutz and Luckmann 1989: 35). The choice between conflicting imaginary projects is basically an act of interpretation. Choosing an imaginary option is an interpretative decision made under the pressure of action and time in an actually present situation (Schutz and Luckmann 1989: 47). The process of

decision itself is a process within the actor's inner duration. Although the choice takes place in the present, it is stamped by the past. Yet its meaning is essentially future oriented. In the process of choosing, knowledge and relevance occur in the form of estimates of practicability and interests in certain future possibilities (Schutz and Luckmann 1989: 35-26). Past and future together determine the values of the weight of a project that are apprehended. Once the weight of the project has been assigned, it can be retained as memory and is used as a comparison with the weight of the other projects – the alternative future. In other words, the actor compares the desirability of one future possibility with the other.

3.3.3.2 Business errors

Entrepreneurs often commit errors during the process of projection or planning. Errors can bring an enterprise a disaster if they are not corrected after detached. However, the nature of errors needs to be understood before a correct prescription can be made. Reason (1990) classifies errors into two types: skill-based slips and lapses, and rule- and knowledge- based mistakes. Skill-based Slips and Lapses are errors that manifest themselves in actions deviating from current intention due to execution failures and/ or storage problems. Rule-and knowledge- based mistakes are made where the agent's plan is inadequate to achieve its desired outcome. Thus, according to Reason's (1990) classification:

1. Slip is a mismatch between intention and action
An example is dialling wrong phone numbers. The intention is satisfactory, but the actions are not carried out as planned. A slip is mainly due to some kinds of attentive failure, and normally occurs in routine situations or over-practiced cases.

2. Lapse involves memory failures
There are three types of lapse: (a) lapse of intention, which concerns with the lost of intention that is under execution; (b) lapse of action, which refers to the failure to trigger the intended action at the proper moment; and (c) lapse of memory, where the intention is specified, but further information necessary to perform the action cannot be retrieved from memory.

3. Rule-based mistake consists of wrong execution of rules or procedures For any task, rules must be selected according to certain criteria of cognitive system to reach a given goal. These include best match and rule strength.[20] Occasionally, rule strength might override other factors resulting in misapplications of otherwise 'good' rules to inappropriate situations.

4. Knowledge-based mistake occurs when a selected plan or intended goal turns out to be not fitted to the problem which is to be solved Knowledge-based mistakes are attributed to the lack of completeness of the mental models used and/or a fault in causal thinking. People are not able to properly recognize the relation between different aspects of the problem or to achieve an adequate diagnosis of the problem. The contexts in which these errors occur are unfamiliar and require diagnostic remedy (Rizzo *et al.* 1994).

The first two types of errors (i.e. skill-based slip and lapse) can be classified as unconsciousness errors due to weak physical capabilities or lacking energy or skills. Such errors can be reduced by technical training. The last two types of error (i.e. rule-based and knowledge-based mistakes) have something to do with uncertainty and hence most relevant to our analysis here. Klein (1999) argues that entrepreneurship and error are theoretical inverses since the function of entrepreneurship, as Knight (1921) argues, is to bear risks and uncertainty. Errors due to uncertainty lead to mismatches of market plans. For Klein, poor exercise of judgement results from one's overlooking something significant. Previous bad judgement has to be revised. Improvement in judgement gives rise to success later. Hence, errors due to uncertainty is genuine economic errors.[21]

3.3.4 Errors due to uncertainty: divergent expectations and entrepreneur's misinterpretation

Entrepreneurs' projections or plans are subject to market tests, depending on the responses of market participants. If entrepreneurs' plans do not meet the expectations in the market, it will result in a financial loss and errors in planning have been committed. Due to structural uncertainty, committing a planning error should not be treated as uncommon in ordinary business life for we never know for sure what will happen in the future, given divergent tastes and expectations and rapidly changing world. An error or a failure

[20] Rule strength is defined to be the number of times a rule has performed successfully in the past.

[21] Economic problems arise out of uncertainty. See Hayek (1945) cited in the next section.

means a business policy does not work in the market and paves way for the revision in the future. Profit or success means a business plan matches the expectations in the market and will become mismatch when outside world changes. Thus, success and failure go hand in hand, each followed by another (Farson and Keyes 2002: 29). Davidsson (2005) correctly claims that the entrepreneurial process is a matching problem.

Success and failure, or matching problem, are associated with time. Hayek (1945) once claims that 'all economic problems are coordination problems, arising out of uncertainty'. A success today can be a disaster tomorrow. Likewise, a failure today can be a success tomorrow. So yesterday's successful experience should not be fully taken as tomorrow's guideline. If we take success and failure as an ultimate end, this will limit our willingness to revise and create (Farson and Keyes 2002: 32). Errors force us to alert to the new situation and to re-examine our way of thinking. Errors allow us to have new insight on the situation. Too much success can be a disaster because policy will be excessively taken for granted. As a result, the entrepreneur may not want to change any policy even when outside world changes rapidly.[22] Success and failure, if viewed as knowledge problems, are manifested in the unexpected change.[23] What is important for the entrepreneur is 'to get the things done' (as cited earlier) through a continuous revision of plans under uncertainty.

The concept of economic error can be further integrated under Hayek's equilibrium framework. Hayek (1945: 47) defines equilibrium as perfect compatibility of plans, a situation that 'the foresight of the different members of the society is in a special sense correct'. However, complete and perfect foresight is most unlikely. Disequilibrium, or mismatches of plans, is therefore a normal phenomenon in the coordination of economic activities.

---

[22] For example, in 1968, Swiss watch craftsmanship led the world and dominated the world market. It occupied 65% and 80% of the world sales and profits respectively. This success made Swiss watch manufacturers unwilling to adopt new technique. In 1967, a Swiss scientist discovered quartz and the Centre Electronique Horloger (CEH) in Neuchâtel developed the world's first quartz wristwatch – the famous Beta 21. Since then, major technical developments followed without interruption: LED and LCD displays, Swatch, quartz wristwatch without battery, etc. The inherent accuracy and low cost of production has resulted in the proliferation of quartz clocks and watches since that time. With generation of pride in craftsmanship, Swiss watchmakers refused to accept quartz technique. Japanese had not pre-occupied with such mentality. They applied this new quartz technique to watch. After ten years, American and Japanese watch output accounts for 8% of the world output while Swiss output declines to only10%.

[23] If changes are expected, events are then fully anticipated, there will be no economic problem.

Given uncertainty, each entrepreneur must consider the planned actions of all other market participants on the basis on his/her own stock of knowledge and exercise judgement. As Knight points out, judgement is liable to err (see above). Wrong judgement or planning mistake in the coordination perspective means that entrepreneurs' plans are unable to come up with the expectation of others. Moving towards equilibrium means closing the gaps of expectations among market participants. It can be concluded that business failure is the first step toward success after errors are eliminated and plans are revised subsequently (Farson and Keyes 2002: 33).

Economic error is viewed as an interpretation problem. Its occurrence forces entrepreneurs to learn and revise their plans if they want their business to be successfully carried out or their products to be accepted by the consumers. The revisions of plans, overtime and divergent expectations in the economy can be converged. If the entrepreneur refuses to accept a mistake and is unwilling to revise plans, he or she is to refuse to accept the social world (i.e. the market). Entrepreneurial learning is thus a process of socialization for market participants to come up with the expectations of others.

3.3.5 Dealing with economic errors: learning, errors elimination and revision of plans

Each time when an error occurs, it indicates no-through road (Farson and Keyes 2002: 75). The driver needs an 'U-turn' and find a way out. Human agents continue to update their expectations in light of the difference between what was expected in the past and what actually happened. When expectation differs from outcome, agents will adjust their actions. The process of re-interpretation constructs new meanings and at the same time reduces uncertainty (Weick 1995: 147). Entrepreneurs learn by trial and error, a measure adopted by most organisms. Karl Popper (1972: 242) argues 'all organisms are constantly engaging in problem solving which "always" proceeds by the method of trial and error; new reactions, new forms, new organs, new modes of behaviour, new hypothesis, are tentatively put forward and controlled by error-elimination'. Entrepreneurial learning is an evolutionary process of cumulative growth of problem-solving knowledge. In Hayek's view, the market is an ongoing, open-ended process of trial and error-elimination, a process in which constantly a number of potential alternative solutions of various kinds of problems are tried out and selected upon through the choices of market participants. It is a process in which new tentative problem solutions are continuously explored, and in which problems themselves are subject to change, as solutions to old problems tend to create new problems. The learning or discovery process involves the history of the entrepreneur's own experience of success and failure. Agents interpret or classify incoming events according to their own experience. Whenever the expectations resulting from the existing interpretation are disappointed, or when beliefs held so far are disproved by new experience, then re-interpretation or reclassification occurs. The whole process of entrepreneurial learning, of the growth of knowledge, is then seen as consisting of such re-interpretation or re-classification, as a process in which our 'frame of reference' is corrected, adjusted, or refined.[24]

Harper's (1994) theory of growth of knowledge casts similar insight on the entrepreneurial learning process. Entrepreneurs are constantly engaged in solving problems which tend to involve much novelty and which are ill-specified (Harper 1994: 56). Whenever actual events diverge from their predictions, decision makers learn that something is wrong with their stock of knowledge. They know that they cannot hold on to their existing conjectural framework (Harper 1994: 63). Simply put, the failure of a plan must be due to inadequate knowledge of the circumstances in which human action has to be taken. Previously unsuccessful policies prompt the need for a revision of plans. A new array of plans is formed, each with a tentative solution to the original problem. The number or variety of proposed solutions is limited by the agents' creativities and imagination (Harper 1994: 71). The new plan too is problematic. Each trial solution is controlled by a process of attempted error elimination. Error elimination is done through testing ideas in practice, which involves the comparison and assessment of rival conjectures in terms of how well they can solve the problems (Harper 1994: 72).

[24] In Lachmann's view (1956, 1970), an entrepreneurial action exists in the form of plans which link with the entrepreneur's stock of knowledge. The interpretation of problematic situation made by the entrepreneur yields provisional judgments to be confirmed later by experience. The formation of plans is a phase in the process of exchange and transmission of knowledge which effectively integrates the outside world. Each plan does not stand alone, but is the result of a series of expectations which have been revised in light of latter experience. These past revisions are the source of present knowledge. On the other hand, the current plans to be revised later as experience accrues are also a source of future knowledge. A new problem situation requires the entrepreneur to invent a new trial solution which is then subject to further testing in the real world. The process continues indefinitely, so that a series of new problems and new plans gradually reinforce in agent's mind. The formation of plans is thus a continuous process, an element of a larger process of the transmission of knowledge.

3.4 Success or failure: profit or loss in the entrepreneurial process

We can now define business success or profit as a result of entrepreneurs' correct judgement or interpretation of the market events. On the other hand, business failure or loss is the result of entrepreneurs' misinterpretation of the market signals. As Von Mises (1949/1966: 291) convincingly argues,

> 'like every acting man, the entrepreneur is always a speculator. He deals with the uncertainty of the future. His success or failure depends on the correctness of his anticipation of uncertain events. If he fails in his understanding of things to come, he is doomed. The only source from which an entrepreneur's profits stem is his ability to anticipate better than other people the future demand of the consumers. If everybody is correct in anticipation the future state of the market of a certain commodity, its price and the prices of the complementary factors of production concerned would already today be adjusted to this future state. Neither profit nor loss can emerge for those embarking upon this line of business'.

Von Mises (1962: 120) argues that it is the entrepreneurial decision that gives rise to profit or loss. 'What makes profit emerge is the fact that the entrepreneur who judges the future prices of the products more correctly than other people do buys some or all the factors of production at prices which, seen from the point of view of the future state of the market, are too low .... On the other hand, the entrepreneur who misjudges the future prices of the products allows for the factors of production prices which, seem from the point of view of the future state of the market, are too high' (Von Mises 1962: 109). Hence, Von Mises (1949/1966: 293) concludes, 'the ultimate source from which entrepreneurial profit and loss are derived is the uncertainty of the future constellation of demand and supply'. Hence, profit and loss serve as a signal for entrepreneurs to interpret and re-interpret market phenomena and allow the ideas of market participants to coordinate.

3.5 Summary

The dynamic model of the entrepreneurial process is summarized in Figure 1. This chapter starts with the axiom that human action has meaning attached to it as human agents make sense out of their everyday business

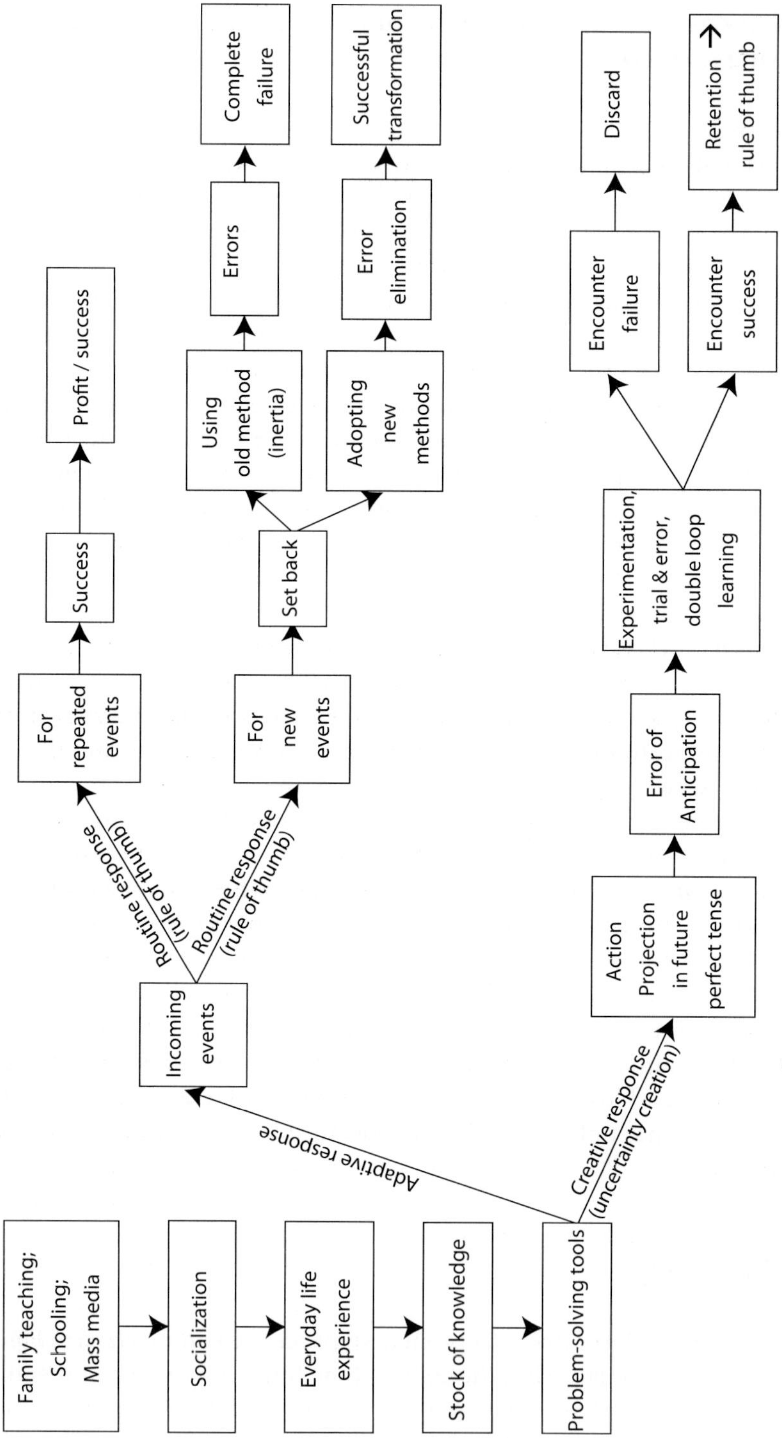

Figure 1. The entrepreneurial process: interpretation, learning, experimentation and error elimination.

life. Experiences from everyday life are accumulated into a stock of knowledge that can be used to interpret incoming events and as problem-solving skills.

If incoming events are repeated and familiar, the entrepreneur can utilize the rule of thumb to solve the problems. Events are anticipated and entrepreneur's plans are consistent with the market participants' expectations. Economic activities are coordinated. The entrepreneur can earn profits using the same stock of knowledge to solve familiar problems.

If incoming events are novel, the established linkages of the mental map will fail to give an adequate account of the new situation. In other words, the stock of existing rules is inapplicable to the new event. The entrepreneur is in a state of conflicting experience. Perceiving novel events, some agents may continue to use old methods to solve new problems. This response does not catch up with the market expectation and is doomed to fail. However, most entrepreneurs will devise new methods if they find that prevailing policies are unable to solve new problems. They learn to adopt new methods by trial and error, and by experimentation. Encountering uncertainty, they will cope with their knowledge-deficiency by creating temporary expectations. This knowledge surrogate will be tested in the market. If this works, then the method will be adopted and routinized as a rule of thumb.

Human action is not seen only as a response to external stimuli. Agents also subjectively and selectively define situations instead of adapting to a ready-made environment. In other words, actors create the environment to which they adapt via experimentation, learning, and trial and error. The process of entrepreneurial planning can be roughly classified into four stages: projecting of an idea, focusing, elaboration of an opportunity and implementing a project. Entrepreneurs' projections or plans are subject to market tests. If plans do not meet expectations in the market, and results in a financial loss, this implies that entrepreneurs have committed errors in planning. Committing an economic error is normal in ordinary business life, given divergent tastes and expectations and rapidly changing world. With uncertainty, each entrepreneur must consider the planned actions of all other market participants based on his/her own stock of knowledge and exercise judgement. Judgement is liable to err. Wrong judgement or planning mistake in the coordination perspective means that entrepreneurs' plans are unable to come up with the expectation of others. The whole entrepreneurial process is thus seen as a process in which our interpretation framework is corrected, adjusted, or refined. Each trial solution is controlled by a process of attempted error-elimination. Business success or profit is the result of entrepreneurs' correct judgement on the market. Business failure or loss is the result of entrepreneurs' misinterpretation of the market signals. In conclusion, profit and loss, originating from uncertainty, serve as signals for entrepreneurs to interpret and re-interpret market phenomena and allow the ideas of market participants to coordinate. As a result, market order emerges spontaneously.

References

Ackermann, R. (1998) Institutional Path Dependence, History and Reform. Paper presented at the EAEPE Annual Conference in Lisbon, 5-8 November 1998.

Allen, M. and R. Haas (2001) The Transition in Central and Eastern Europe: The Experience of Two Resident Representative. In: *Transition Economies: How Much Progress.* IMFstaffpapers, volume 48, Special Issue. Washington DC, USA: IMF, pp. 9-28.

Berger, P. and B. Berger (1976) *Sociology: A Biographical Approach*, revised edition. Middlesex, UK: Penguin.

Berger, P. and T. Luckmann (1966) *The Social Construction of Reality.* New York, USA: Anchor Books.

Boland, L.A. (1982) *The Foundations of Economic Method.* London, UK: George Allen & Unwin.

Cauthorn, R.C. (1989) *Contributions to a Theory of Entrepreneurship.* New York, USA: Garland Publishing Co.

Chen, Y-C., W.M.H. Tsai and M-J.J. Lin (2006) An Exploratory Study of Key Factors to Trigger Entrepreneur Rebound from Business Failure. *Journal of Entrepreneurial Research*, vol. 1 (1), 45-74 [text in Chinese].

Davidsson, P. (2005) The Entrepreneurial Process as a Matching Problem. In: *Proceedings Academy of Management Conference*, Hawaii.

DeBono, E. (1980) *Opportunities.* Middlesex, UK: Penguin.

DeBono, E. (1992) *Serious Creativity.* New York, USA: Harper Business.

Farson, R. and R. Keyes (2002) *Whoever Makes the Most Mistakes Wins: The Paradox of Innovation.* New York, USA: The Free Press.

Fleetwood, S. (1995) *Hayek's Political Economy: The Socio-economics of Order.* London, UK: Routledge.

Gifford, S. (1992) Allocation of Entrepreneurial Attention. *Journal of Economic Behavior and Organization*, vol. 19, 265-283.

Harper, D.A. (1994) A New Approach to Modelling Endogenous Learning Processes in Economic Theory. In: P. Boettke, I. Kirzner and M. Rizzo (eds.) *Advances in Austrian Economics I.* Greenwich, USA: JAI Press, pp. 49-79.

Hayek, F.A. (1945) The Use of Knowledge in the Society. *American Economic Review,* vol. 35, 519-30, reprinted in F.A. Hayek (1947) *Individualism and Economic Order,* London, UK: Routledge, pp.77-91.

Hayek, F.A. (1952) *The Sensory Order.* Chicago, USA: University of Chicago Press.

Hisrich, R.D., M.P. Peters and D.A. Shepherd (2005) *Entrepreneurship.* 6 ed. New York, USA: McGraw-Hill Irwin.

Jones, S. (1987) Choosing Action Research: A Rationale. In: I.L. Mangham (ed.) *Organisation Analysis and Development.* New York, USA: John Wiley, pp. 234-254.

Kirzner, I.M. (1973) *Competition and Entrepreneurship,* Chicago: University of Chicago Press.

Klein, D.B. (1999) Discovery and the Deepself. *The Review of Austrian Economics,* vol. 11 (1-2), 47-76.

Knight, F.H. (1921) *Risk, Uncertainty, and Profit.* New York, USA: Houghton Mifflin.

Knight, F.H. (1956) *On the History and Methods of Economics.* Chicago, USA: The University of Chicago Press.

Lachmann, L.M. (1956) *Capital and its Structure.* Kansas City, USA: Sheed Andrews and McMeel, Inc.

Lachmann, L.M. (1970) *The Legacy of Max Weber.* London, UK: Heineman.

March, J.G. and H.A. Simon (1958) *Organisation.* New York, USA: John Wiley.

Minniti, M. and W. Bygrave (2001) A Dynamic Model of Entrepreneurial Learning. *Entrepreneurship: Theory and Practice,* vol. 25 (3), 5-16.

Popper, K. (1972) *Objective Knowledge: An Evolutionary Approach.* Oxford, UK: Oxford University Press.

Reason, J. (1990) *Human Error.* Cambridge, UK: Cambridge University Press.

Rizzello, S. (2000) Economic Change, Subjective Perception, and Institutional Evolution. *Metroeconomica,* vol. 51 (2), 127-150.

Rizzo, A., D. Ferrante and S. Bagnara (1994) Handling Human Error. In: J.M. Hoc, P.C. Cacciabue and E. Hollnagel (eds.) *Expertise and Technology: Cognition & Human-Computer Cooperation.* Hillsdale, USA: Lawrence Erlbaum, pp. 195-212.

Rogers, E.M. (1983) *Diffusion of Innovations,* 3rd edition. New York, USA: The Free Press.

Schumpeter, J.A. (1934/1961) *The Theory of Economic Development.* New York, USA: Oxford University Press.

Schumpeter, J.A. (1943) Capitalism, *Socialism and Democracy.* London, UK: Allen and Unwin.

Schumpeter, J.A. (1947) The Creative Response in Economic History. In: R. Clemence (ed.) (1951) *Essays of J.A. Schumpeter.* Cambridge, USA: Addison-Wesley, pp. 216-226.

Schutz, A. (1970) *On Phenomenology and Social Relations*, Chicago: The University of Chicago Press.

Schutz, A. and T. Luckmann (1989) *The Structures of the Life World.* Vol.II. Evanston, USA: Northwestern University Press.

Shackle, G.L.S. (1958) *Time in Economics.* Connecticut, USA: Greenwood Press.

Vesper, K.R. (1990) *New Venture Strategies.* 2nd edition. New Jersey, USA: Prentice Hall.

Von Mises, L.V. (1949/1966) *Human Action: A Treatise on Economics,* 3rd edition. Chicago, USA: Contemporary Books.

Von Mises, L.V. (1962) Profit and Loss. In: *Planning for Freedom.* South Holland, USA: Libertarian Press, pp.112-150.

Weick, K. (1969) *The Social Psychology of Organising.* Reading, USA: Addison-Wesley.

Weick, K. (1995) *Sensemaking in Organisations.* Thousand Oaks, USA: Sage.

Weigert, A.J. (1981) *Sociology of Everyday Life.* New York, USA: Longman.

White, L.H. (1977) Uncertainty and Entrepreneurial Expectation in Economic Theory. Unpublished Senior Honours Thesis, Harvard College, 31 March 1977.

Wu, R-L., S-F. Wang and T-K. Hsu (2009) A Dynamic Perspective on Entrepreneurs' Mental Changing Process during Entrepreneurial Transitional Stage. *Journal of Entrepreneurial Research*, vol. 4 (1), 1-31 [text in Chinese].

Chapter 4. National capabilities

4.1 A need for a new research agenda

As mentioned in Chapter 2, the production function approach in the mainstream neoclassical paradigm has found not very fruitful in understanding economic development of a country. Essentially, the traditional Solow's growth models ignore knowledge and learning. Aware of this deficiency, Romer (1994), Grossman and Helpman (1991) and, Aghion and Howitt (1998) attempt to broaden the Solow's growth model by including knowledge or human capital in their analysis. With the presence of increasing returns, the new exogenous growth models suggest that countries can develop along their own growth path, rather than convergence as suggested by the old growth theories. However, this revised model, though popular, does not provide us with a deep understanding of the development process (Metcalfe 2001).

In recent decades, evolutionary economics has gained ground. In particular, Schumpeterian scholars in the capabilities school and national innovation systems approach[25] have contributed tremendously to our understanding of economic development. Unlike neoclassical models of the firm and growth, these two paradigms emphasize the role of technology, knowledge and learning problems in economic growth.[26] There is little doubt that as a description of reality, the evolutionary approach is far more superior than the production function approach. Despite being closer to the reality in their treatment of economic issues than their neoclassical school counterpart, the two paradigms have not put human agency at the forefront of economic analysis. Specifically, the capabilities school uses firm as an unit of analysis[27] while national innovation systems focus on the national level. As a result, the fundamental problems of

[25] For a review of the concepts of national systems of innovation, see Lundvall (1997).

[26] For a comparison of the role of technology in economic development between neoclassical and evolutionary paradigms, see Metcalfe (2001).

[27] The problem of using firm as a unit of analysis has been identified by Metcalfe (2001: 13) who notes: 'To speak of the knowledge base of any organization is problematic for what is known is individual, what is understood is social and a matter of organization and intercommunication.'

economic development, namely uncertainty and coordination problems encountered by human agents, have not been adequately addressed. It cannot be denied that technological innovation plays an important role in economic development. However, technology and its applications should be interpreted and assessed from the 'first person' point of view (Addleson 1995), rather than from an 'omnipotent' third party perspective.[28] Only viewed from the actor's perspective can we fully identify economic problems. As a humanistic science, this chapter argues that all economic analysis should be built upon human agency. Based on this premise, in this chapter, we shall construct a theory of national capabilities in the Austrian subjectivist perspective. Adopting the 'first person' perspective, this chapter starts from an individual human agency level and explains economic capabilities based on the Schutzian theory of human action (Schutz 1970). This subjectivist perspective is then extended to understand firms, and national capabilities and competitiveness. In what follow, the foundation of national capabilities is explained in terms of agent's stock of knowledge. The interactions between acting agents (such as entrepreneurs and employees) will create organizational culture and determine firm capabilities and industrial growth. Finally, through competition and market interactions among firms in the industry as well as interactions between producers and consumers, institutions and business cultures will gradually emerge. This social stock of knowledge, as a result of the long term evolutionary process, will in turn determine national capabilities and competitiveness in global markets. While this chapter recognizes the influence of institutions on firms' decision making, unlike contemporary evolutionary literatures, the Austrian subjectivist perspective argues that all institutions are also the consequence of the coordinating effort of human agents which attempt to interpret external events or make sense out of social or economic interactions. Such a perspective will be used to understand some controversial issues in economic development.

4.2 Foundation of national capabilities

An economy is made up of people who act. National capabilities therefore derive from agents' capabilities which are defined as a pool of knowledge an agent possesses in order to solve problems and/or create new things.

[28] We do not deny scientific knowledge, or in our case, the effect of technology on economic development. All objective factors have to be assessed by human minds when making a decision. Thus, subjectivism, as a method is perfectly consistent with objective science. See O'Driscoll and Rizzo (1985: 42).

Where does this knowledge come from? The answer is that it is accumulated from an agent's everyday lived experience during the process of perception, interpretation and learning.

4.3 Formation of agent's capabilities: experience and interpretation

Max Weber and Alfred Schutz argue that as human agents make sense of their everyday life, they attach a meaning to actions at the same time (Weick 1969). Action is essentially inter-subjective, since all human agents find their experiences necessarily reaching out of the existence of other persons. Making sense of the external world means interpretation. Hence, 'interpretation is a process of perceiving the other and his or her interaction within symbolic frameworks so that we can make some sense out of what the other is doing ...' (Weigert 1981: 74).

Experiences from everyday life are accumulated into a stock of knowledge that can be used to interpret incoming events. When we experience, our knowledge and capabilities grow. Experiences enter the individual's consciousness via daily contact with our parents, face-to-face interaction with friends and neighborhood, watching television and movies, etc. These lived experiences are then typified and crystallized into routines or the rules of thumb which can be used as a skill or problem solving technique in everyday life. The stock of knowledge, originating from the actor's lived experiences, is a device for receiving external information and organizes itself into patterns. Once the patterns are formed, the framework will be used as a broad catchment area for interpreting incoming events which involves a sorting of new experiences into existing categories, sometimes adds or modifies the structure as a result. As soon as the agent encounters an external event, the mind will trigger the established interpretative channel and has access to all knowledge (meaning) associated with that event (DeBono 1980: 14). In short, the stock of knowledge developed in our mind allows us to make sense of the world. Without such a system, capabilities to solve problems would be impossible.

4.4 Capabilities to innovate

The stock of knowledge which an agent possesses helps to identify and solve problems, as well as to innovate. This stock is by no means homogeneous

(Schutz 1970: 74). Because of diverse experiences, human agents will respond differently to the same objectively defined stimulus (O'Driscoll and Rizzo 1985: 38-39; Yu 1999). Men in identical situations may act differently because of their different views of the future (Lachmann 1970: 36). In simple terms, the cognitive patterns are not symmetrical. The lack of symmetry gives rise to new ideas and creativity (DeBono 1992: 15).

Innovation is a learning process. Human agents are not passive robots. They do not only adapt themselves to the external world but also adjust the environment to their needs through deliberate and conscious choices. Besides being diffusers and users of knowledge, agents are also a source of knowledge. In other words, they are a builder and user of knowledge, creator of economic possesses and above all, the engine of change (Hayek 1952; see also Rizzello 1999). Human agents constantly create reasons for their own existence, trying to have as much influence as possible and thus to determine as much as possible the future states of the world in a direction that favors their own development (Rizzello 2000: 127-150). Often, some human agents can see things differently and are able to move out of the routine track and create. Modifying the categories of their framework (Lane *et al.* 1996), or in some cases even adding a new category, some individuals are able to give others a different sense of the meaning through re-creation. Simply put, they are 'sense-givers' (Thayer 1988: 250, 254). Creative activity thus involves the shifting of all different sets of reference frames that would usually be ordered differently and be seen as incompatible – until something clicks into place as a new way of looking at how things fit together. Such discovery means that the actor escapes from the existing patterns of interpretation and reorganizes ideas into new sequences (DeBono 1992: 15). The innovator always 'embodies the possibilities of escape from what might otherwise appear to us to be incomprehensible, or from what might otherwise appear to us to be a chaotic, indifferent, or incorrigible world' (Thayer 1988: 250, 254).

4.5 From individual agent to firm capabilities

The nation's capabilities or national innovation systems reflect firm capabilities which are in turn based on capabilities of individuals and the way in which individual members interact. Individuals do not produce alone. They are engaged in team production. Each person sees things differently as well as possesses different capabilities or knowledge. How can production be possible such that entrepreneurs can realize their economic plans? How can costs be saved in coordinating thoughts of many individuals? The basic solution is to increase the understanding of other persons' actions and thus increase the chances of success in coordination (Yu 1999). This can be done by setting up a formal organization called the firm. The founder(s) of the firm, by trial and error, experiments a set of rules which generally lay down clear lines of authority and communication with the intention of ensuring that the entrepreneurial goal may be attained (Silverman 1970: 14). The newly established firm is initially characterized by a pattern of relationships which is less taken-for-granted by the participants who seek to coordinate and control. By asking the members to subordinate their in-order-to motives to the officially defined goals, the firm 'attempts de facto to substitute an objective context of meaning for the subjective configuration in which the individual actor discovers the meaning of his (or her) action' (Jehenson 1973: 227). The world taken for granted inside the firm is thus composed of actors following typical courses of action prompted by a set of invariant, typical motives. In other words, employees are given expectations about appropriate acts for themselves and others in various status positions. As a result, they are then able to apprehend the meanings associated with economic actions of other people and to form a self based view on the responses of others. Members will meet the expectations of others because these expectations are part of the definitions of themselves (i.e. they have been internalized). A system would remain unhindered in its function if the members could retain their reciprocal anonymity and interact only at the level of 'they' relationship (Jehenson 1973: 229). In essence, they conform to a set of shared values which is central to the existence of a firm (Silverman 1970: 131). In this way, the founder of the firm creates a 'communicative common environment' (Schutz 1970: 31, 165). It is a situational environment shared by a group of people who are able to communicate with one another. Treating the firm as an entity that supports shared mental constructs, Foss (1997) rightly remarks that 'an important part of the rationale of firms is that it makes sense out of the world for a subset of the economy's input-owners by cultivating a shared knowledge-base that promotes the coordination of the plans of these input-owner in the face of change'. By establishing a firm, the entrepreneur is in fact building a coherent world of knowledge[29] and a cultural community (Schutz 1970: 81).

[29] Schutz (1970: 80) argues that the world of knowledge is incoherent, only partially clear and not free from contradiction.

4.6 Capabilities to cooperate and coordinate

The common communicative environment created by the entrepreneur becomes firm's culture or in Nelson and Winter's (1982) terms 'routine'.[30] This routine, which is the firm's capabilities, is the rule of thumb which enables the firm to solve problems and save costs of coordination. In many occasions, a firm needs to cooperate with another firm in order to learn new technology and share knowledge. Cooperation can help firms to lower costs, grow and compete in the global market. Since firms possess different stocks of knowledge and routines, attempt to cooperate with another organization will give rise to interpretation and hence coordination problems. The capability for the firm to cooperate with another firm implies its ability to interpret actions of the members of another organization correctly and make appropriate judgement. When a firm cooperates with another *local* firm, communication and coordination may not be a big problem for both firms interpret each other action in the same cultural framework. However, when a local firm cooperates with a foreign firm, interpretation problems arise for both firms do not share the same culture. Often, firms in certain countries are deeply embedded in their cultures that their foreign partners may find huge difficulties in understanding their actions and cooperate with them. When members of these joint ventures are unable to make correct interpretation, then coordination fails. A successful international cooperation requires both parties to explore, learn and adjust to each other. It has cost implications. The interpretation problems and coordination costs explain why some firms may perform well in a domestic setting but cannot do well overseas. It also explains why there are various forms of cooperative arrangements and organizations in international business, and why in certain situations, a firm prefers a joint venture to foreign direct investment.[31]

---

[30] Nelson and Winter (1982) conceptualize firms as possessing path-dependent knowledge bases called routines. They develop a behavioral theory of the firm beyond its origin as a short term analysis of firm behavior, into a more long term analysis of how the firms within an industry adapt to new environments through a process of search for new and more profitable routines.

[31] In recent decades, there is a growing literature applying transaction costs economics to explain various forms of international cooperation (for example, see Casson 1982; Anderson and Gatignon 1986; Hennart 1991; Hennart and Reddy 1997). My arguments are complementary to the new institutional economic approach. For an institutional analysis of transnational entrepreneurship in international business, see Yeung (2002: 29-61).

4.7 National capabilities and competitiveness

National capabilities are peoples' ways of doing things. They are 'social' stock of knowledge[32] embodied in firm routines and originated in peoples' minds. National capabilities are governed by rules and institutions. As Lundvall (1992: 10) notes, 'institutions provide agents and collectives with guide-posts for action ... Institutions make it possible for economic systems to survive and act in an uncertain world'. Explaining the difference in national capabilities, or the difference in national competitiveness, is to explain the difference in institutions which are the result of the long term evolutionary process. Since each firm possesses its own routine, how can firms' own routines evolve into national capabilities, and result in national competitiveness? The answer is that all successful firm strategies have to be passed through market tests and selections.

4.8 Emergence of national capabilities: international competition, market selection and rule-following

Entrepreneurs' business strategies are subject to market tests. Profitability governs the market selection. Under competition, those options which happen to lead to profits will survive and be retained. Those options which happen to lead to losses will be discarded. Once a business plan is found profitable or feasible, imitators will adopt it. In other words, the new ways of doing things are adopted and gradually evolved into national capabilities.

The emergence of national capabilities can be explained in the Popperian perspective. Entrepreneurs of firms are constantly engaged in solving problems which tend to involve much novelty and which are ill-specified (Harper 1994: 56). What is learned may be 'false' and entrepreneurs may fail. The market system is a system of profit and loss. Whenever actual events diverge from predictions, entrepreneurs learn that something is wrong with their stock of knowledge. They know that they cannot hold on to their existing conjectural framework (Harper 1994: 63). Simply put, the failure of a plan must be due to inadequate knowledge of the circumstances in which the action has to be taken. Previously unsuccessful plans prompt the need for a revision of plans. A new array of plans is formed, each with a

[32] Since knowledge cannot exist outside human mind, the so called 'social' stock of knowledge is therefore only a shorthand way of referring to those institutions, customs or norms which people in an economy commonly adopt in solving a problem.

tentative solution to the original problem. The number or variety of solutions proposed is limited by the entrepreneur's creativity and imagination. The new plan is problematic too. Each trial solution is controlled by a process of attempted error-elimination. Error elimination is done through the testing of ideas in practice, which involves the comparison and assessment of rival conjectures in terms of how well they can solve the problems (Harper 1994: 72). Successful plans are adopted and imitated in the market. Reinforced by rule-following, new ways of doing things or national capabilities gradually emerge. National capabilities or the rules of thumbs are the resultant of millions of entrepreneurs' learning processes and market selections.

Hayek argues that the limits of our reason require us to follow rules. Rules are the device for coping with our ignorance (Hayek 1967: 90). They facilitate the making of decisions in complex situations. They limit our range of choice by reducing the list of circumstances which we need to take into account in particular circumstances, singling out certain classes of facts as alone determining the general kind of action which we should take (Hayek 1964: 11). Hence, 'rules ... thus do not govern only our actions. They also govern our perception, and particularly our perceptions of other people's actions' (Hayek 1962: 45). 'Rules of doing things' can be regarded as common schemes of behavior, which simplify the complexity of the world and enable us to operate with a certain degree of predictability. They standardize people's ways of doing things and help to solve problems. Different individuals act inside the world and within its limits, which ensure order and certain regularity through simplification. These rules, reflecting the culture of a region, govern national capabilities and international competitiveness. In summary, it can be concluded that all firms within an economy are likely to share some common behavioral and organizational features due to their embeddedness in a common institutional context (Dosi and Malerba 1996: 15). As will be illustrated in the next section, the persistent difference in firm and hence national capabilities is due to the difference in institutions, social stock of knowledge and people's perception.

4.9 Understanding national capabilities through the subjectivist lens

We can now summarize what has been argued. If economic development involves creative activities hitherto not yet thought of as well as the adjustment of prevailing experience, then it is of utmost importance to bring human agency back to development economics. Schumpeterian scholars in the capabilities school or in the national innovation systems approach have done excellent jobs in correcting many drawbacks of the mainstream neoclassical analysis. These scholars focus on the significance of technology in economic development (e.g. Dosi and Orsentigo 1988; Freeman 1990; Metcalfe 2001). Concepts such as technological capabilities, opportunities, trajectories and transformation are used to explain the development path of an economy. The subjectivist approach, on the other hand, centers human agency and formally puts human knowledge and ignorance at the forefront of the analysis via the first person approach. This approach enables us to be free from 'technological determinism'. It starts with the human agency and examines the agent's economizing efforts on the evolution of the firm, industry and whole economy. In this regard, the causes of a phenomenon in the economy can be traced back to its component industries, firms and ultimately to human agents.[33] Thus this approach has a micro-macro link. Moreover, individuals, firms and human institutions are interactively related. Metcalfe (2001) rightly notes that all changes of knowledge come from human thought. National capabilities ultimately come from individual and yet each individual value and decisions are shaped by his/her social value and environments. In many cases, collective actions with good initial intentions may end up in bad or disastrous result. This is the unintended consequence of human economizing actions (Menger 1883/1985). The unintended consequence of human actions has been the experimental characteristics of the mind process. There is no single experience, hence, no single suite of strategies that can speak for all and consequently, no single path to economic development. Nevertheless, our subjectivist approach is able to throw lights on development issues addressed in the evolutionary tradition. For example, 'how and why do nations differ in their productive capabilities and hence, rate of economic growth?' and 'how can and why do national capabilities develop at different rates over time for different nations?' (see Metcalfe 2001: 21). In this chapter, we attempt to understand some important development issues in the subjectivist perspective: the role of social stock of knowledge in economic development, the nature of 'shock therapy' policy in economic reforms and the role of non-searchable knowledge in economic development.

1. National capabilities, deriving from the social stock of knowledge, are a crucial factor in economic development. Such capabilities or knowledge, originating from agent's lived experiences, help to get things done, to solve

[33] Von Mises (1949/1966: 18) argues that human action 'cannot be traced back to its causes. It must be considered as an ultimate given and must be studied as such'.

economic problems and to innovate. It is a kind of problem-solving skill. No matter how clumsy these skills are, without them, things cannot be done. More importantly, learning cannot be done in a vacuum mind. It depends on prior knowledge.[34] Before we learn, we need an initial pool of knowledge. This prior knowledge is gained in our childhood via family, school and socialization. The more a person experiences, the richer the stock of knowledge an individual possesses. Hence, the faster the speed of learning is, the quicker the solutions will be found. In the national terms, it means a higher growth rate. As we have mentioned above, the agent's pool of knowledge is a device of receiving external information and organizes itself into patterns. Once the patterns are formed, the knowledge reservoir will be used as a broad catchment area for interpreting incoming events. When an actor faces a familiar problem, he or she is able to handle it without much thinking. It saves the costs of learning of solving problems. Therefore, it makes sense to claim that an older person is usually wiser.[35] More importantly, each technique in the stock of knowledge has its biography. Each skill is historically linked with past experiences. So using a single technique to solve a problem today means that the actor is using many knowledge learned through his/her early years. Moreover, such knowledge are not only gained through his/her lifetime but also from the actor's ancestors and are passed on to the actor. Hence, the older the race is, the wiser the nation is. The subjectivist view of national capabilities explains why some nations can learn and grow faster than others. This argument is illustrated by the 'East Asian miracles' (World Bank 1993). In particular, East Asian economies such as Singapore, Malaysia, Taiwan, Hong Kong and Thailand have been economically enhanced by overseas Chinese (Redding 1990). The Chinese merchants in these regions have been equipped with a long history of Chinese cultures. Their 'Chinese' pools of trade knowledge enabled them to operate well in terms of small family business dynamics. Comparatively, other ethnic groups in the same regions could not compete with these Chinese family businesses. Applying our arguments, those minds which inherit Chinese business culture and knowledge are capable of saving time in learning and in problem-solving. On the other hand, many natives or non-Chinese ethnic groups may need to struggle through a long mental process of learning before it can solve a

[34] Metcalfe (2001: 20) notes that learning depends on experience.

[35] As will be noted below, an old person is less likely to change the way of thinking. Nationally, this impedes innovation and economic growth.

small problem. In short, the argument is that experience and knowledge count in economic growth.[36]

2. While national capabilities, or social stock of knowledge, can help to foster growth, they can also hinder growth. In neo-Schumpeterian literatures, resistance to change is largely explained by the concept of path dependence, organizational inertia and lock-in effects and that history matters in explaining a country's backwardness (Arthur 1989; David 1995). Our subjectivist perspective casts light on institutional inertia or resistance to change too. Persistence of an old system is fundamentally associated with mental thinking. As mentioned, the society's total stock of knowledge is a product of mental interpretation, reclassification and learning. Agents' interpretation process has a certain time sequence that allows thinking to follow a routine perception track. In other words, agents see things in a certain way and expect things to be worked out in a certain way. Once the incoming information is organized into a (mental) pattern, then the agent no longer has to analyze or categorize incoming information. All that is required is to have enough information to trigger the pattern. The mind then follows along the pattern automatically in the same way as a driver follows a familiar road. Over time, a habit develops because the actor simply uses his or her interpretation system routinely. Resistance to change means that actors' thinking is locked up in old interpretation structures, concepts and institutions (DeBono 1992: 17). Two further points are worth to mention. Firstly, once agents take the stock of knowledge for granted, then perception becomes even more important, because the way they look at a situation will determine what they can do about it. Secondly, unless another competing pattern is developed in the agent's interpretation framework, anything similar to the established pattern will be treated just as if it were that pattern. It is just like the watershed to a valley. Unless there is a competing valley, water will gather into the centre of the single valley. Furthermore, when economy's stock of knowledge is seen as a product of social construction, rules or moral norms are then followed relatively unconditionally since the behavior prescribed by them is considered as 'right'. If individuals violate these rules, then they will have a 'bad conscience'. Hence, an institution is reinforced during the process of socialization when individuals learn to behave according to the 'right' rules of the game that constitute the society they live in (Ackermann 1998).

[36] Such argument has nothing to do with racial superiority. The argument here is that experience counts. Of course, it remains to explain why some natives, who have lived for so long, are unable to learn and modernize in order to compete in the world market.

It may be argued that in order to prevent institutional inertia, whenever interpreting incoming events is necessary, actors should not take their experience or knowledge for granted. Unfortunately, as Allen and Haas (2001: 25) notes, all psychological change is very hard to bring about. It is often the case that individuals are unwilling to let go of existing concepts, perceptions or institutions in order to put both previous and recent experiences into a new perspective. As explained above, rule-following has its merits. After a period of time, as the pattern in agents' minds survives for too long, it will become non-separable and resisted disruption. In other words, over time each piece of knowledge works together as an integrated part of the thinking pattern, and is reinforced by social norms, customs and routines. By that time, changing patterns will become extremely difficult (DeBono 1992: 17). Unless there is radical thinking which revolutionizes the way of doing things, old thinking will persist as long as agents take experiences for granted unconditionally and interpret the external world in a routine manner.

We can illustrate our arguments by referring to a famous modernization programme in the Chinese history, namely Westernization or Self-Strengthening Movement (1870-95) in the Ch'ing Dynasty. After the Opium War, the Ch'ing government was amazed by advanced technologies of foreign gunboats and cannon. China's officials at that time perceived that it was imperative to buy and learn to build arsenals from foreign countries. The underlying argument was to adopt superior techniques of the Westerners to curb the Westerners. However, the program ended up in a huge waste of resources. While there are many reasons for the failure, such as bureaucratic inefficiency, corruption and nepotism,[37] the most important one is that technology cannot be forcefully imposed. China under the Ch'ing government still remained, both economically and intellectually, in extremely backward conditions. The economy was pre-dominantly agricultural and the society was generally closed from the outside world. More devastatingly, cultural triumphalism and moral superiority had made China a reluctant improver and bad learner (Landes 1999: 336). Foreign science, astrology and technologies at that time were regarded by Chinese high officials and old mandarins as miseries, bizarre and evils (Guo 1986: 34). The government enterprises, though engaging in a modern way of production, retained old-style managerial and administrative practices. What they produced were either imitated or outdated machines. Ships and guns produced were no where comparable in quality to their Western

[37] The theory of rent seeking in public choice can contribute to understanding this phenomena.

counterparts. Eventually, the programme was terminated altogether after the coup failure in 1898, led by the pro-reformed Emperor Guangxu. National capabilities are socially embedded. They cannot be forcefully transferred without altering the social stock of knowledge, or more precisely, people mentality. Hence, our arguments are consistent with Archibugi and Michie (1995: 3) which notes,

> 'technology is not easily transferable across countries but, on the contrary, is country-specific and rooted in skills, capabilities and knowledge which in turn are accumulated through time. Nations differ not only in the quantity of innovations introduced, but also in the methods by which these innovations are adopted and in their sectoral composition'.

It took China brutal revolutions, civil wars and turmoils (such as the overthrow of the Ch'ing monarchy by Sun Yat-Sen in 1911, May Fourth Movement in 1919 and Mao's communist revolution in 1949) for Chinese to unlearn old things before China could embark on the road of modernization via Deng's open door policy in the 1980s. In short, a nation with thinking deeply rooted in the traditional value requires a longer period of time to learn new things and modernize.

3. If we accept the argument that economic development is a matter of change in mental perception, then our framework can shed light on the understanding of one kind of reform paths, namely the shock therapy, denoted by the reform in Russia. Unlike the gradualist approach in China, the shock therapy policy (or big-bang strategy) requires people to give up entirely all their existing stocks of knowledge at *one* time. Actors totally unlearn old ways of doing things and learn new things in a very short period of time. This involves revolutionary unlearning.[38] In Russia, it means that people abandoned all communist teaching which they had taken for granted for many years and accepted capitalists' ways of doing things.[39] This had created a shock in the mental process. Russian suddenly found that their stocks of knowledge were unable to solve their daily problems. In other words, shared expectations vanished. Coordination failed. As a

[38] Revolutionary learning can be seen as 'a process of deinstitutionalization or unlearning in which anomalies with established knowledge embedded in structuration principles and properties are discovered' (Stein 1997: 737).

[39] An old way of thinking is a strong desire for equal distribution of income. Another example is speculation. Speculation was also regarded as a criminal activity and was condemned. On the other hand, in Commonwealth of Independent States countries, no living memory of a market economy remains. For a review of old ways of thinking, see Allen and Haas (2001: 12).

result, production and economic activities were in chaos. This explains the fact that in transition economies of Central and Eastern Europe, the Baltics, Russia, and the other countries of the former Soviet Union, output fell by more than 40% on average (Fischer 2001). Such real output loss was accompanied by severe dislocations, large redistribution of income, and severe income losses by many people. Given the dramatic fall in the output and suffering from extreme hardship during the reform, a lot of Russians with their old interpretation framework being still in force in their minds may perceive that it would be easier to cope with everyday life under the communist system than in the transition stage. Therefore, some of them started to miss their good old Bolshevik days. Their minds still strongly valued economic stability and desired security under the communist regime (Weisskopf 1997: 309-327). This explains why some Russian resisted the economic reform. To reiterate, a successful economic reform requires a change in mentality. After all, a human institution is not 'an objective physical phenomenon, but a human mental construct' (Stein 1997: 730). On this, a policy reform package aims to help people to learn new things are of utmost importance.

References

Ackermann, R. (1998) Institutional Path Dependence, History and Reform. Paper presented at the EAEPE Annual Conference in Lisbon. 5-8 November 1998.

Addleson, M. (1995) *Equilibrium versus Understanding.* London,UK: Routledge.

Aghion, P. and P. Howitt (1998) *Endogenous Growth Theory.* Cambridge, USA: MIT Press.

Allen, M. and R. Haas (2001) The Transition in Central and Eastern Europe: The Experience of Two Resident Representative. In: *Transition Economies: How Much Progress.* IMFstaffpapers, Volume 48 (Special Issue), Washington DC, USA: IMF, pp. 9-28.

Anderson, E. and H. Gatignon (1986) Modes of Foreign Entry: A Transaction Cost Analysis and Propositions. *Journal of International Business Studies,* vol. 17 (Fall), 1-26.

Archibugi, D. and J. Michie (1995) The Globalisation of Technology: A New Taxonomy. *Cambridge Journal of Economics,* vol. 19 (1), 243-256.

Arthur, W.B. (1989) *Increasing Returns and Path Dependence in the Economy.* Ann Arbor, USA: University of Michigan Press.

Casson, M.C. (1982) Transaction costs and the theory of multinational enterprise. In: A.M. Rugman (ed.) *New Theories of the Multinational Enterprise*. London, UK: Croom Helm, pp. 10-28. Reprinted in P.J. Buckley and M.C. Casson (1985) *The Economic Theory of the Multinational Enterprise*, London, UK: Macmillan, pp. 20-38.

David, P.A. (1995) Clio and the Economics of QWERTY. *American Economic Review*, vol. 75, 332-237.

DeBono, E. (1980) *Opportunities*. Middlesex, UK: Penguin.

DeBono, E. (1992) *Serious Creativity*. New York, USA: Harper Business.

Dosi, G. and F. Malerba (1996) Organizational Learning and Institutional Embeddedness. In: G. Dosi and F. Malerba (eds.) *Organization and Strategy in the Evolution of the Enterprise*. London, UK: MacMillan, pp.1-26.

Dosi, G. and L. Orsentigo (1988) Technological Regimes and Firm Behavior. In: G. Dosi and F. Malerba (eds.) *Organization and Strategy in the Evolution of the Enterprise*. London, UK: MacMillan, pp.42-71.

Fischer, S. (2001) Ten Years of Transition: Looking Back and Looking Forward. In: *Transition Economies: How much Progress*. IMFstaffpapers, volume 48 (Special Issue), Washington DC, USA: IMF, pp.1-8.

Foss, N. (1997) Austrian Insights and thc Theory of the Firm. *Advances in Austrian Economics*, vol. 4, 175-198.

Freeman, C. (1990) *The Economics of Innovation*. Aldershot, UK: Edward Elgar.

Guo, T.Y. (1986) *Jin Dai Zhong-guo Shi Gang* [*The Recent History of China*]. Hong Kong, China: The Chinese University Press, volumes 1: 19th century; volume 2: 20th century [text in Chinese].

Grossman, G. and E. Helpman (1991) *Innovation and growth in the global economy*. Cambridge, USA: MIT Press.

Harper, D.A. (1994) A New Approach to Modelling Endogenous Learning Processes In Economic Theory. In: P. Boettke, I. Kirzner and M. Rizzo (eds.), *Advances in Austrian Economics I*, Greenwich, USA: JAI Press.

Hayek, F.A. (1952) *The Sensory Order*. Chicago, USA: University of Chicago Press.

Hayek, F.A. (1962) Rules, Perception and Intelligibility. *Proceedings of the British Academy*, vol. XLVIII, 321-344, reprinted in: F.A. Hayek (1967) *Studies in Philosophy, Politics and Economics*, New York, USA: Clarion Book, pp. 43-65.

Hayek, F.A. (1964) Kind of Order in Society. *New Individualist Review*, vol. 3 (3), 3-12.

Hayek, F.A. (1967) *Studies in Philosophy, Politics and Economics*. New York, USA: Clarion Book.

Hennart, J-F. (1991) The Transaction Costs Theory of Joint Ventures: An Empirical Study of Japanese Subsidiaries in the United States. *Management Science*, vol. 37 (April), 483-497.

Hennart, J.-F. and Reddy, S. (1997) The Choice between Mergers/Acquisitions and Joint Ventures: the Case of Japanese Investors in the United States, *Strategic Management Journal*, 18: 1-12.

Jehenson, R. (1973) A Phenomenological Approach to the Study of the Formal Organisation. In: G. Psathas (ed.) *Phenomenological Sociology Issues and Applications.* New York, USA: John Wiley, pp. 219-247.

Lachmann, L.M. (1970) *The Legacy of Max Weber*. London, UK: Heinemann.

Landes, D. (1999) *The Wealth and Poverty of Nations.* New York, USA: W.W. Norton.

Lane, D., F. Malerba, R. Maxfield and L. Orsenigo (1996) Choice and Action. *Journal of Evolutionary Economics*, vol. 6, 43-76.

Lundvall, B.A. (1992) *National Systems of Innovation: Towards a Theory of Innovation and Interactive Learning.* London, UK: Printer.

Lundvall, B.A. (1997) National Systems and National Styles of Innovation. Paper presented at the 4th International ASEAT Conference: Differences in styles of technological innovation, Manchester, 2-4 September 1997.

Menger, C. (1883[1985]) *Investigations into the Method of the Social Sciences with Special Reference to Economics.* New York, USA: New York University Press.

Metcalfe, J.S. (2001) Technology and Economic Development: A Comparative Perspective. Background paper for Industrial Development Report 2002/03, New York, USA: United Nations Industrial Development Reports.

Von Mises, L. (1949/1966) *Human Action: A Treatise on Economics,* 3rd edition. Chicago, USA: Contemporary books.

Nelson, R.R. and S.G. Winter (1982) *An Evolutionary Theory of Economic Change.* Cambridge, USA: Harvard University Press.

O'Driscoll, G. jr. and Rizzo, M.J. (1985) *The Economics of Time and Ignorance.* London, UK: Blackwell.

Redding, S.G. (1990) *The Spirit of Chinese Capitalism*. Berlin, Germany: de Gruyter.

Rizzello, S. (1999) *The Economics of the Mind.* Aldershot, UK: Edward Elgar.

Rizzello, S. (2000) Economic Change, Subjective Perception, and Institutional Evolution. *Metroeconomica*, vol. 51 (2), 127-150.

Romer, P. (1994) The origins of endogenous growth. *Journal of Economic Perspectives,* vol. 8, 3-22.

Schutz, A. (1970) *On Phenomenology and Social Relations.* Chicago, USA: The University of Chicago Press.

Silverman, D. (1970) *The Theory of Organisations.* London, UK: Heinemann.

Stein, J. (1997) How Institutions Learn: A Socio-Cognitive Perspective. *Journal of Economic Issues*, vol. XXXI (3), 729-740.

Thayer, L. (1988) Leadership/communication: A Critical Review and a Modest Proposal. In: G.M. Goldhaber and G.A. Barnett (eds.), *Handbook of Organisational Communication*. Northwood, USA: Ablex, pp. 231-263.

Weick, K.E. (1969) *The Social Psychology of Organising.* Cambridge, USA: Addision-Wesley.

Weigert, A.J (1981) *Sociology of Everyday Life.* New York, USA: Longman.

Weisskopf, T.E. (1997) Economics Without History: The Effort To Westernize The East. In: N. Aslanbeigui and Y.B. Choi (eds.), *Borderlands of Economics: Essays in Honor of Daniel R. Fusfeld.* London, UK: Routledge Press.

World Bank (1993) *The East Asian Miracle: Economic Growth and Public Policy.* Oxford, UK: Oxford University Press.

Yeung, H.W-C. (2002) Entrepreneurship in International Business: An Institutional Perspective. *Asia Pacific Journal of Management,* vol. 19, 29-61.

Yu, T.F-L. (1999) Toward a Praxeological Theory of the Firm. *Review of Austrian Economics,* vol. 12 (1), 25-41.

Chapter 5. Innovation and communication

'Without audience, art is incomplete'[40]

5.1 Introduction

In human history, some geniuses' works were unappreciated in their lifetime. For example, Évariste Galois' mathematical contributions were finally published and declared correct in 1843, eleven years after his death.[41] Gregor Mendel, who is now known as the 'father of modern genetics', published his paper in 1866. The paper, now a seminal work in genetics, had little impact to the scientific community at that time (Henig 2000).[42] The paper was cited only about three times over the next thirty-five years since it came out! It was not until the early 20th century that the importance of his ideas was realized.[43] In the art world, Vincent Van Gogh's career life is a tragedy. He produced an incredible number of masterpieces that live for the rest of human history. It is hard to imagine that his paintings were sold as scraps at Breda flea market for around 5 cents in 1903.[44] During his short but turbulent life, he sold only one painting for 400 francs, just 4 months before his death.[45]

---

[40] Http://xcis-pro.com/favorite.html.

[41] Http://en.wikipedia.org/wiki/genius.

[42] The scientific community at the time believed that pangenesis were responsible for inheritance. For example, Darwin's theory of evolution used pangenesis instead of Mendel's model of inheritance (Henig 2000).

[43] In 1900, Mendel's contribution was rediscovered by Hugo De Vries and Carl Correns (Henig 2000).

[44] Http://www.forbes.com/lifestyle/2003/11/25/cx_1125hot.html.

[45] http://bonniebutterfield.com/vincentvangogh.htm. Given that Van Gogh had never sold any painting successfully before, as an economist, it is interesting to speculate who was the buyer of Van Gogh's painting, 'The Red Vineyard'. There are two possible buyers: either this buyer is another genius who appreciates Van Gogh's talent or this buyer buys Van Gogh's painting on the philanthropic ground. If the reason is the latter one, then it is reasonable to speculate that this buyer is his brother Theodorus who continually and selflessly provided financial support to Van Gogh throughout Van Gogh's lifetime. However, source supports the former. It is reported that the buyer was Anne Boch, also a painter, who bought 'The Red Vineyard' in Brussels for 400 francs (http://www.nicks.com.au/index.aspx?link_id=76.1257). It is also reported that Ms. Boch loved to promote young artists including Van Gogh whom she admired for his talent.

Some geniuses are more 'lucky'. Albert Einstein achieved an unprecedented level of reception in the scientific community.[46] Michelangelo was never the disregarded man. He was often showered with attention and admiration by the community for his artistic talent. His remarkable talent has led him to be recommended to the Ruler of Florence. Likewise, Pablo Picasso's and Salvador Dali's[47] talents were recognized by their contemporaries.

In economics, Ronald Coase is now regarded as the founder of new institutional economics. His paper *The nature of the firm* was not well received when it appeared in 1937. Only in 1960, 23 years later, when he published another paper 'The problem of social cost' that his 1937 insight was rediscovered. His contribution was fully recognized when he received the Nobel Prize in 1991. Although the award comes lately,[48] Coase is lucky to be a Nobel laureate in Economic Sciences because the Prize is only awarded to a living scholar.

The issue this chapter tries to address is: why some new ideas and innovations are readily accepted by the community at large, while others take a very long time to be recognized. No doubt, culture, social and political backgrounds play important roles in this regard. In management of innovation literature, the acceptance of a new idea can be viewed in terms of diffusion of innovation. In his seminal work, *Diffusion of Innovations*, Rogers (1962/2003) defines the diffusion of innovation as a process by which an innovation is communicated, diffused and adopted

[46] According to a report, Albert Einstein's 1905 paper was ignored by the physics community. This began to change after he received the attention of just one physicist, perhaps the most influential physicist of his generation, Max Planck, the founder of the quantum theory. Soon, owing to Planck's laudatory comments and experiments that gradually confirmed his theories, Einstein was invited to give lectures at international meetings, such as the Solvay Conferences, and he rose to fame rapidly in the academic world. After he presented his paper on November 6, 1919, the headline of *The Times* of London read, 'Revolution in science – New theory of the universe – Newton's ideas overthrown – Momentous pronouncement – Space 'warped'. Almost immediately, Einstein became a world-renowned physicist, the successor to Isaac Newton. Invitations came pouring in for him to speak around the world. In 1921. Einstein began his first world tour, visiting the United States, England, Japan and France. Everywhere he went, the crowds numbered in the thousands (http://www.britannica.com/eb/article-256584/albert-einstein).

[47] During World War II, Dali took refuge in the United States, returning after the war's ended in Spain. His international reputation 'continued to grow, based as much on his flamboyance and flair for publicity as on his prodigious output of paintings, graphic works, and book illustrations; and designs for jewelry, textiles, clothing, costumes, shop interiors, and stage sets' (http://www.rain.org/~artworks/dali/history.html).

[48] Albert Einstein was nominated for and denied the Nobel Award eight times between 1910 and 1921 (http://www.pentrace.net/penbase/data_returns/full_article.asp?id=466).

through different channels over time among communities (see also Rogers and Shoemaker 1971). He highlights five factors that influence the rate of adoption of a new product. They are relative advantage, compatibility, degree of complexity, trialability and observability (see also Yu and Robertson 1999: 76-97). These characteristics will help to persuade potential adopters to embrace or reject an innovation. Rogers' theory is confined to a new physical product. However, in the art world such as oil painting, a new vision, expressed by brush on canvas, exhibits no physical attributes. Artworks involve aesthetics and are highly abstractive and subjective in nature.

This chapter seeks to explain the acceptance of a new idea from an intersubjective perspective, with special reference to creativity in art.[49] I shall argue that whether a new idea, such as in oil painting, is accepted or not by the community is a matter of understanding, or more precisely, subjective interpretation. In what follows, I shall introduce the concepts of intersubjective understanding based on Max Weber and Alfred Schutz. Then using oil painting as an illustration, I shall apply the theory to explain why some artists' new ideas are accepted immediately and why some receive cold receptions. The issue involves two interactive parties, namely, the innovator in the social world and members in the community who try to understand the innovation. Furthermore, I shall explain why a radical technological innovation is more difficult to be accepted by the public than an incremental innovation and why creativity in art is more difficult to be accepted than scientific discovery. The last section presents the concluding remark.

5.2 The innovator in the social world

No individual can exist except in relationships with others, just like we cannot learn any language without other speakers. Human agents live, act and create in the social world. As Max Weber (1921/1968: 562) argues, all human actions are oriented towards the behaviors of others. Building on Weber, Alfred Schutz argues that 'a man sees that others act just as

[49] Creativity in painting is deliberately chosen in this study. Scientific innovations, such as in mathematics or chemistry, can be tested 'objectively' against the physical world and hence, its acceptance can be based on its applicability or practicability. Unlike scientific innovations, a judgment on a painting involves aesthetic and is highly subjective. Acceptance of a painting can hardly be tested objectively in terms of applicability or practicability. It bases on judgments of sentiment and taste.

he does, just as he also sees that others treat him as an actor' (Schutz and Luckmann 1989: 7). Hence, an action 'is, in any case, reciprocal' (Schutz and Luckmann 1989: 72). Action anticipates an inter-subjective future – one's own subjective future and other people's subjective future (Schutz and Luckmann 1989: 85). Artists have their audiences before them subconsciously when creating an artwork. We perceive 'in another's mind some thought of our appearance, aims, character, friends, and so on, and are variously affected by it' (Weick 1995: 22). A painter may paint an object existing in the physical world. While doing so, he or she orients his/her inner thought towards others' using his or her brushes on canvas. By conveying messages to others, he or she attempts to persuade the community to appreciate his or her vision. Hence, it is true to claim that 'without audience, art is incomplete'. Similarly, scientists attempt to convince others by their new theories, although they deal with laws of nature. After a novel idea is delivered, whether it is accepted or not by the community is a matter of understanding, or more correctly, subjective understanding. It is rather impossible for a person to accept an idea without understanding. If I fully understand your work, this means my experience of the world is same as yours. Hence, you and I share the same 'communicative common environment' (Schutz 1970: 31).

5.3 Constructing the unknown future

Human agents are not passive robots. They do not only adapt themselves to the external world but also adjust the environment to their needs through deliberate and conscious choices. Besides being diffusers and users of new ideas, agents are also a source of novelty. In other words, they are the builders of new knowledge, creators of the new world and above all, engines of change (Hayek 1952/1976; see also Rizzello 1999; 2000). Jones (1987: 24) argues that human agents do not only respond to external stimuli, but subjectively and selectively define situations. In other words, human agents 'enact' rather than just 'react' to environment (Jehenson 1973: 235; Jones 1987: 24). As Weick (1969: 27) argues, 'instead of adapting to a ready-made environment ..., actors themselves create the environment to which they adapt'. Using their imaginative powers, actors form new perception to the outside world, unlearn the learned and unlock mental inertia, initiate a disturbing force to the human world. The change in the world view is thus connected with the fact that human agents constantly create the reasons for their own existence, try to have influence as much as possible and thus determine the future states of the world in a direction that favors their own development as much as possible (Rizzello 2000: 127-150). This is the foundation of innovation.

Human agents construct unknown, but not insensible, future (Weick 1995: 4). Applying Thayer's (1988: 250, 254) argument, it can be said that an innovator is 'the one who gives others a different sense of the meaning of that which they do by recreating it in a different form, a different face, in the same way that a pivotal painter or sculptor or poet gives those who follow him (or her) a different way of seeing ...'. The innovator is a sense-giver, always embodying 'the possibilities of escape from what might otherwise appear to use to be incomprehensible, or from what might otherwise appear to use to be a chaotic, indifferent, or incorrigible world' (see also Weick 1995: 10). Innovation, or sense-making, implies the construction of something which is sensible to the social world.

5.4 Accepting an innovation: intersubjective understanding

The prerequisite for accepting an innovation is to understand it. If a novel idea is not understood, we cannot expect it to be accepted. When a human agent encounters a novel idea originating from another person, he or she will try to make some senses out of it. Making sense of the external world means understanding. In the subjectivist perspective, understanding the external world is to interpret the meaning of the novel idea.

How can an understanding be possible in the social world? The answer is that an action is essentially intersubjective, since all human agents find their experiences necessarily associated with other persons. Everyday life builds on the category of the 'other' (Weigert 1981: 55). Individuals find themselves related to the surrounding world in order to create a meaningful life and share it with others. People are taken to be 'other I's' just as I am experienced as an 'another you'. Only in this way, 'we' can make sense. Subjective understanding or interpretation, as Weigert (Weigert 1981: 74) puts it, 'is a process of perceiving the other and his or her interaction within symbolic frameworks so that we can make some sense out of what the other is doing ... If we cannot make any sense out of the other's interaction, it may be that there is no sense in it, or worse, it may be that there is no sense in me'.

Interpretation of the world is based on the stock of knowledge which is accumulated from everyday life through learning from school, teaching from parents and socialization from mass media or interaction with friends (Schutz 1962: 7). This knowledge at hand functions as a scheme of reference. The experiences of the external world, such as mountain, church, custom, law and war, are pre-defined and taken for granted. I may never see a chestnut tree but if I see one, I know that it is a tree and in particular a tree, showing all the familiar features of a typical tree. I may ask what kind of tree this is? The question presupposes that a chestnut tree is different from all other kinds of trees which I know.[50] These experiences form the base of our expectations. For example, we expect animals with certain features of a dog as dogs. If an innovator, artist or scientist, deliberately violates our experienced self by doing something radically different from the past, then our sense of reality is also violated. This violation threatens the sense of underlying reality which grounds our world taken for granted as the basis for everything else. The uncertain self may seek a possible alternative explanation in order to make sense out of the problematic situation. If none of the solutions works, then the innovator will be seen as a threat to the society and his or her product will be rejected. Some creative thinkers are even condemned by the public as deviants. We can conclude that if a new idea is consistent with our experiences, it then will be accepted. Further away from our experiences, the idea will not be recognized. Paradoxically, if we are familiar with an innovation, this implies that the innovation is trivial and consists of nothing new.

5.5 Understanding Picasso's paintings

Painters do not live alone in the world. They do not only paint for their own, but also paint for others in the social world. Painters try to send their visions of life to the community by their brushworks. When an artist paints a tree, he or she tells the world that the object is a tree (or more correctly *his* or *her* tree). Of course, each painting has its meaning attached to it. There are many ways to paint a tree. A naturalist painter would portray a tree as close as the real world one. The painting consists of a trunk, leaves, stems, roots, perhaps, flowers and fruits too. Because it looks like real, people can easily identify the object as a tree from their experiences, and appreciate this painting from their stock of knowledge accumulated from everyday life. Such traditional way of drawing a tree is taken for granted and therefore widely accepted. People will have no conflict of knowledge when seeing this picture. An experienced but non-creative painter may

[50] In his classic work, *The Sensory Order*, Hayek (1952/1976) explains the perception process in term of classification problem exercised in human minds. See Yu (2007).

use sophisticated skills, such as color, shade and light, to portray a tree. People can still identify this tree if it is drawn in a traditional way. In other words, they accept this painter's product and skills without doubt. Every painting is then a 'looking glass self' product. Put differently, the concept of a tree held by the community is same as the artist. If everyone draws a tree as such, there is no surprise, no novelty, no innovation. However, this painting is generally accepted, though the meaning manifested in the drawing is trivial.

The art world is a highly imaginative one. Artists subjectively define the future for themselves and the general public to adapt. A German philosopher, Martin Heidegger (1993) highlights this point in his work, *The origin of the work of art* as below: 'Works of art are not merely representations of the way things are, but actually produce a community's shared understanding. Each time a new artwork is added to any culture, the meaning of what it is to exist is inherently changed.'[51] To be unique, a creative painter would not draw a tree as what a tree 'usually' looks like. By drawing a tree in different manner, the painter adds new meaning to the art world. This is what Pablo Picasso did.

Pablo Picasso is one of most recognized masters of the art in the 20th century and regarded as an innovator in oil painting.[52] Before Picasso, painters had been obsessed with the 19th-century Naturalism in which painting is about the 'reality of vision.' People at that time only supported factual and realistic representation of the subject. Their minds registered naturalistic painting as real.

Picasso was born as a creative painter. He once remarked, 'God is really only another artist. He invented the giraffe, the elephant and the cat. He has no real style. He just goes on trying other things.'[53] Picasso did not like to follow the tradition. He claimed, 'If one knows exactly what is going to be done, why do it?' Furthermore, he said, 'there are painters who transform the sun into a yellow spot, but there are others who, thanks to their art and intelligence, transform a yellow spot into the sun.' Confronting with Naturalism, Picasso created the 'impossible.' He did not follow the trivial way of painting. He said, 'I do not evolve, I am.' He re-defined the future artwork for the world to evolve. A history in oil painting was made. As a

[51] See http://en.wikipedia.org/wiki/theoriginof_theworkofart.

[52] He was also a sculptor, printmaker, ceramicist and stage designer.

[53] All quotes from Picasso in this paper are retrieved from the BrainyQuote website (http://www.brainyquote.com/quotes/quotes/p/pablopicas397437.html).

result, Picasso introduced a new painting technique that revolutionized European painting in the early 20th century. This technique is referred in art history to as Cubism.[54]

What Picasso attempted to do was to break away from the restriction of academic art by disregarding the traditional way of using color and light. He experimented with line and form. Instead of viewing objects from a single angle, Picasso depicted the subject from multiple angles simultaneously as an attempt to present the subject in the most complete way. In his paintings, objects were broken up, analyzed and reassembled in an abstracted form. Often the surfaces of the facets or planes intersect at angles that show no recognizable form. In particular, in one of his oil painting, 'Woman in an armchair' of 1913, Picasso intentionally distorted the woman body into an amoeba-like shape. Furthermore, 'her head, body and limbs are exaggerated and deformed almost beyond recognition. The jumble of patterns, and strong lines of the wainscoting and floor, convey an unsettling tension that is at odds with placid, gray-and-white profiles that float like cast shadows upon the surface. Through such a juxtaposition of tension and calm, the artist depicted the several faces of emotion that form the reality of human existence'(http://www.groveart.com/index.html).

During the process of innovation, Picasso's vision was directed to other people as a painter in the society. In other words, Picasso, as a painter, was socially circumscribed (Schutz and Luckmann 1989: 70). He saw things with the assumption that others saw things as himself. However, the community might not see things as Picasso did. This rendered 'understanding problems'. Picasso created the world in which he assumed the same as the world other people saw. Artists who interpreted oil paintings in the 19th-century lens initially found it hard to accept Picasso's novel style. Picasso's new technique entered into others' minds as a new event. Members in the community tried to interpret Picasso's new technique and make sense out of his paintings. However, they had no similar stock of knowledge in their minds as the one in Picasso's. Two

[54] The Cubist movement began in 1906 with Pablo Picasso and Georges Braque who lived in the Montmartre quarter of Paris, France. Cubism influenced artists of the first decade of the 20th century. It gave rise to the development of new trends in art like futurism, constructivism and expressionism. Innovative artists, Braque and Picasso, sought new ways to express space and form in painting. Cubism does not aspire to real vision, but to the artist's mental experience of the world. Thus a new 'writing of the real' (Kahnweiler) was developed, put into practice by Braque and Picasso first in the so-called Analytical phase which is dominated by a 'reality of conception', to which the representation of the world submits (http://www.gamelow.com/painters-c/cubist.php).

possibilities will occur: some people who could not comprehend Picasso's paintings would try to protect themselves by rejecting it as evil and cranky.[55] Others, encountering something totally novel, would cope with their knowledge-deficiency by creating a knowledge surrogate (White 1977: 80). This knowledge surrogate can be regarded as a temporary interpretation on novel painting, waiting for the community consensus or approval (which is a typification process in Schutz's term; see Schutz 1962: 15-19). This process takes time. Understanding and accepting Picasso's paintings is thus a process of collective typification. As some members in the community began to understand Picasso's new technique, Picasso, with full confidence, continued to put forward his novel idea by producing more daring paintings. His works were more colorful and expressive than ever. From 1968 through 1971, he produced a series of paintings and hundreds of copperplate engravings. These works were dismissed by some members in the community as pornographic fantasies of an impotent old man or 'the incoherent scribbling of a frenetic old man'.[56] However, Picasso's vision slowly gained ground and was steadily comprehended by his peer group. Eventually, Picasso's path-breaking method in oil painting was fully 'understood' and branded as 'neo-expressionism' after his death. While it is right to say that Picasso is ahead of his time, it is more correct to say that it takes time for the community to interpret and integrate his novel ideas into prevailing interpretation frameworks of the society.

5.6 Implications

Two further implications can be drawn from the above discussion. First, it can be argued that radical technological innovation is more difficult to be accepted than incremental innovation. Second, creativity in art is more difficult to be accepted than scientific discovery.

5.6.1 Radical breakthrough versus adaptive innovation

David Galenson (2010) divides two types of artists: conceptual innovators, who make radical innovations in their field at a very early age; and experimental innovators, whose innovations develop slowly over a long

---

[55] This is the case in the late Ching dynasty when government officials in the imperial China first time contacted with foreign technologies that they did not understand. With fear, they condemned those technologies as miseries, bizarre and evils and therefore should be shielded off (Yu and Kwan 2003: 75).

[56] Http://www.edinformatics.com/great_thinkers/picasso.htm.

period of experimentation and refinement. In economics literatures, conceptualists conduct radical innovation and experimentalists deal with adaptive or incremental innovation. Radical innovation is an extraordinary discovery (Dosi and Fagiolo 1997: 11). This type of innovation, in Schumpeter's sense, exercises 'creative destruction' to the society (Schumpeter 1934/1961). In Schumpeterian innovation, the agent is concerned with doing things drastically different from the past (Kirton 1984: 137). According to Schumpeter (1934/1961), this type of innovation can only be understood ex post but it can practically never be understood *ex ante*; i.e. it cannot be predicted by applying ordinary rules of inference from pre-existing facts. O'Driscoll and Rizzo (1985: 67) further remark, this type of innovation depends on 'the capacity of seeing things in a way which afterwards proves to be true, even though it cannot be established at the moment. This creative leap cannot be conclusively established because it literally leaps over the requisite logical steps'. Contrary to Schumpeterian innovation, adaptive or incremental innovation is an ordinary discovery. It largely leaves social and economic systems unchanged. This kind of activity is concerned with 'doing things better'. It adapts to changing environment (Loasby 1989: 178). This category broadly includes those activities such as gap filling, imitation, pattern duplication and model perfection. Bill Gates' breakthrough in information technology (IT) belongs to Schumpeterian innovation. Asian computer manufacturers such as Acer or Samsung that improve or perfect IT/computer industries by producing cheaper and more user-friendly models belong to adaptive innovation. These two types of innovative activities have different implications on subjective understanding and hence on acceptance. Schumpeterian innovation deliberately violates peoples' expectation. It follows that a sense of reality at the centre of individuals' self is also violated (Weigert 1981: 75). Peoples' stocks of knowledge are now unable to tackle new problems brought about by radical technological breakthrough. Experience hitherto taken for granted becomes problematic (Schutz 1970). Selection of an appropriate response to a drastic change involves not only responding to one novel event associated with one action, but also drawing upon a record of past associations (Fleetwood 1995: 115). If people can link a novel event to previously experienced events in their interpretation framework, then a radical innovation can be accommodated. Without this capacity, people would be incapable of comprehending any kind of novel behavior (Fleetwood 1995: 112). If the innovation is truly radical, it is difficult for people to link the novel events with their existing stocks of knowledge. On the other hand, it is relatively easier for people to link an incremental innovation with their previously experienced events in their interpretation framework. In the perspective of subjective understanding, we can conclude that an incremental innovation is relatively easier to be understood and accepted by the community than a radical technological breakthrough.

5.6.2 Scientific breakthrough versus creativity in art

It can be argued that accepting a scientific breakthrough is easier than creativity in art because the former can be 'objectively' tested (see note 49). If a scientific theory is tested to be valid, then the community will unanimously accept it. However, this point cannot be unduly taken. As Stephen Hawking (1988) explains, 'No matter how many times the results of experiments agree with some theory, you cannot be certain that the next time the result will not contradict the theory'. Popper (1963) forcefully argues that the truth of our theories, even the best theories, cannot be verified by scientific testing, but can only be falsified. For at one time, people believed that the sun revolved around the earth. It is now known as 'wrong'. Similarly, in future, the sun may be found not at the centre of the solar system. Growth in knowledge is subject to 'conjectures and refutations' (Popper 1963).[57] In other words, it is 'in the interplay between the tentative theories (conjectures) and error elimination (refutation) that scientific knowledge advances toward greater and greater problems'[58].

While not denying the role of scientific testing in the growth of human knowledge, this chapter argues that creativity in art is more difficult to be understood by the community than a theoretical breakthrough in natural science due to the unique nature of art. According to Schutz (1962), natural science has a twofold aim. First, the production of a theory which agrees with experience and second, the explanation of common-sense concepts of the nature. Hence, a scientist has to develop devices by which the thought objects of common-sense perception are superseded by the thought objects of science (Schutz 1962: 4). All our knowledge of the world, both common sense and scientific, involves constructs. Strictly speaking, there is no such thing as an objective fact. All facts are the facts selected from universal context by the activities of our mind. Hence, all facts are always interpreted as facts (Schutz 1962: 5). It is up to the natural scientists to

[57] According to Karl Popper, 'science does not advance by repeated attempts at confirmation of hypotheses. Rather it involves endless testing, the constant overthrow of existing scientific theories and their replacement by wholly new and better kinds of knowledge, that is, the new systems of theories of ever greater content' (Harper 1996: 61).

[58] See http://en.wikipedia.org/wiki/karl_popper.

determine which parts of the universe of nature, which facts and events are relevant to their research purposes. These facts are neither pre-selected nor pre-interpreted. In other words, they do not 'reveal intrinsic relevance structures' (Schutz 1962: 5). Whereas in creativity in art, observational fact or social world is essentially structured. It has a particular meaning and relevance structure for human agents who have pre-selected and pre-interpreted their world by a series of common sense constructs of the reality of everyday life. The thought objects constructed by the artists are built upon the thought objects constructed by the common sense thought of human agents living their everyday life in the community. Hence, the constructs used by an artist are 'constructs of the constructs' made by acts on the social scene. those behavior the researcher tries to explain according to the procedural rules of their science. A scholar in natural science does not need to know the biography of a scientist in order to understand a physical law while understanding the meaning of an artwork, we need to go into the biographical history of the artist. Therefore, an understanding of Vincent Van Gogh's painting requires insight into his turbulent life, because his style of painting is demonstrated by a projection of the painter's inner experience through brushwork. In Van Gogh's own words: 'What lives in art and is eternally living, *is first of all the painter*, and then the painting' [italics added]. Hence, to understand an Expressionist artist we must first explore their own biography (http://bonniebutterfield.com/vincentvangogh.htm). To put differently, subjective understanding needs to be conducted in the 'first person perspective' (Addleson 1995). In this particular case, Van Gogh's paintings can only be fully understood from Van Gogh's perspective. Since knowing the biography and thinking of a person is a very complicated process, therefore, it takes a long time for the community to accept an artist's contribution. On the contrary, in scientific discovery, one needs not go into the biography and the mind of a scientist in order to understand his or her contribution. In conclusion, it is relatively easier for us to understand an innovation in science than creativity in art.

5.7 Conclusion

This chapter seeks to explain the acceptance of a new idea from a phenomenological perspective, with special reference to creativity in art. The chapter has argued that whether a new idea, such as in oil painting, is accepted or not by the community is a matter of subjective understanding. Based on human agency theories given by Max Weber and Alfred Schutz, this chapter has argued that innovators, like other human agents, act in the social world. Instead of adapting to a ready-made environment, innovative artists themselves create the environment to which they will adapt. By recreating the artwork in different forms, they add new meanings to the social world. The prerequisite for the community to accept an innovation is to understand it. Members of the community will attempt to make sense out of the creative artwork. If an innovator deliberately violates our experienced self by doing something radically different from the past, our sense of reality will be violated. The uncertain self may seek a possible alternative explanation to make sense out of the problematic situation. Two possible outcomes can be mentioned. After the process of typification, the innovation may be eventually understood and accepted, though it may take a long time. However, it may be the case that the creativity cannot be understood at all. As a result, the innovator is seen as a threat to the society and condemned as deviants. The arguments developed in this chapter help us to understand the creative world of Pablo Picasso and his success in the world of art. Although this chapter is largely confined to artwork, the arguments can be extended to scientific innovation. Further research is called for.

References

Addleson, M. (1995) *Equilibrium Versus Understanding: Towards the Restoration of Economics as Social Theory.* London, UK: Routledge.

Coase, R. (1937) The Nature of the Firm. *Economica*, vol. 4, 386-405.

Coase, R. (1960) The Problem of Social Cost. *Journal of Law and Economics*, vol. 3, 1-44.

Dosi, G. and G. Fagiolo (1997) Explaining the Unknown on Entrepreneurship, Coordination and Innovation Driven Growth. International Institute for Applied System Analysis Report, IR-97-077, October.

Fleetwood, S. (1995) *Hayek's Political Economy: The Socio-economics of Order.* London, UK: Routledge.

Galenson, D.W. (2010) Understanding Creativity. NBER Working Paper 16024.

Harper, D.A. (1996) *Entrepreneurship and the Market Process: An Inquiry into the Growth of Knowledge.* London, UK: Routledge.

Hawking, S. (1988) *A Brief History of Time.* New York, USA: Bantam Books.

Hayek, F.A. (1952/1976) *The Sensory Order.* Chicago, USA: University of Chicago Press.

Heidegger, M. (1993) *Basic Writings. 'On the Origin of the Work of Art.'* 2nd edition. New York, USA: Harper Collin's Press.

Henig, R.M. (2000) *Monk in the Garden: The Lost and Found Genius of Gregor Mendel, the Father of Genetics*. Orlando, USA: Houghton Mifflin Harcourt.

Jehenson, R. (1973) A Phenomenological Approach to the Study of the Formal Organisation. In: G. Psathas (ed.) *Phenomenological Sociology Issues and Applications*. Hoboken, USA: John Wiley, pp. 219-247.

Jones, S. (1987) Choosing Action Research: A Rationale. In: I.L. Mangham (ed.) *Organisation Analysis and Development*. Hoboken, USA: John Wiley.

Kirton, M.J. (1984) Adaptors and Innovators. *Long Range Planning*, vol. 17 (2), 137-143.

Loasby, B.J. (1989) A Subjective Appraisal of Austrian Economics. In: B.J. Loasby, *The Mind and Method of the Economist*. Aldershot, UK: Edward Elgar.

O'Driscoll Jr., G.P. and M. Rizzo (1985) *The Economics of Time and Ignorance*. Oxford, UK: Blackwell.

Popper, K. (1963) *Conjectures and Refutations: The Growth of Scientific Knowledge*. London, UK: Routledge.

Rizzello, S. (1999) *The Economics of the Mind*. Aldershot, UK: Edward Elgar.

Rizzello, S. (2000) Economic Change, Subjective Perception, and Institutional Evolution. *Metroeconomica*, vol. 51 (2), 127-150.

Rogers, E.M. (1962/2003) *Diffusion of Innovations*, 5th edition. New York, USA: Free Press.

Rogers, E.M. and F.F. Shoemaker (1971) *Communication of Innovations: a Cross-Cultural Approach*, 2nd edition. New York, UK: Free Press.

Schumpeter, J.A. (1934/1961) *The Theory of Economic Development*. New York, USA: Oxford University Press.

Schutz, Alfred (1962) *Collected Papers I: The Problem of Social Reality*. M. Natanson (ed.), The Hague, the Netherlands: Martinus Nijhoff.

Schutz, A. (1970) *On Phenomenology and Social Relations*. Chicago, USA: The University of Chicago Press.

Schutz, A. and T. Luckmann (1989) *The Structures of the Life World*. Vol. II. Evanston, USA: Northwestern University Press.

Thayer, L. (1988) Leadership/communication: A Critical Review and a Modest Proposal. In: G.M. Goldhaber and G.A. Barnett (eds.) *Handbook of Organisational Communication*. Northwood, USA: Ablex, pp. 231-263.

Weber, M. (1921/1968) *Max Weber on Law in Economy and Society*. M. Rheinstein (ed.), Translated by E. Shils and M. Rheinstein. New York, USA: Simon and Schuster.

Weick, K. (1969) *The Social Psychology of Organising*. Reading, USA: Addison-Wesley.

Weick, K. (1995) *Sensemaking in Organisations*. Thousand Oaks, USA: Sage.

Weigert, A.J. (1981) *Sociology of Everyday Life*. New York, USA: Longman.

White, L.H. (1977) Uncertainty and Entrepreneurial Expectation in Economic Theory. *Unpublished Senior Honours Thesis.* Harvard College, USA.

Yu, F-L.T. (2007) Entrepreneur's Interpretation, Innovation and Coordination in Austrian Subjectivist Perspective. *Global Business and Economics Review*, vol. 9 (2/3), 255-270. (Special Issue on Applied Behavioural Economics).

Yu F-L.T. and D. Kwan (2003) Learning, Catching Up and International Economic Order: Trilateral Relationship between China, Britain and Hong Kong in the Entrepreneurial Perspective. In: *East Asian Business Systems in Evolutionary Perspective: Entrepreneurship and Coordination.* New York, USA: Nova Science, pp. 67-88.

Yu, F-L.T. and P.L. Robertson (1999) Austrian and Evolutionary Perspectives on Consumer Demand and Firm Strategy. In: S.C. Dow and P.E. Earl (eds.) *Economic Organisation and Economic Knowledge: Essays in Honour of Brian Loasby*, Volume I. Cheltenham, UK: Edward Elgar, pp. 76-97.

Chapter 6.
Economics of international trade

6.1 The foundation of neoclassical international trade theory

The history of the development of the theory of international trade is an interesting one. It is not unusual to conceive that economists would first develop a theory of exchange based on two individuals of the same country and then applies the theory to international transactions.[59] However, it is not the case in the history of economics. Early classical economists (such as Adam Smith and David Ricardo), being hampered by the canon of the labor theory of value, were not able to formulate a general theory of exchange based on two individuals in the same country. On the contrary, the theory of international trade, in which the labor theory of value cannot be applied, has often been the pioneer and inventor of the new analytical tools which later are applied to the general theory of exchange (Haberler 1961: 99).

Early writers, Aristotle and Thomas Aquinas, did not write on international trade, though they presented a set of moral standards for market exchanges. With the emergence of nation-states in the late middle ages, trade with other countries became a topic of particular interest to economic thinkers and practitioners. Mercantilism as a form of economic nationalism emerged in the 17th and 18th centuries Europe. It represents the earliest attempt to describe the function of international trade. Promoting economic nationalism, we are not surprised that mercantilist thinkers examined international trade from a 'national perspective'. Hence, theories of international trade with 'nation' as a unit of analysis opens up the Classical School tradition.

In *The Wealth of Nations* 1776, Adam Smith presents his arguments on foreign trade as follows: 'If a foreign country can supply us with a commodity cheaper than we ourselves can make it, better buy it of them with some part of the produce of our own industry, employed in a way

[59] Strictly speaking, it is neither possible nor essential to distinguish the theory of international trade with the theory of domestic trade (Haberler 1961: 55). As will be seen, my criticisms on neoclassical international trade theories can well be applied to the general theory of exchange.

in which we have some advantage' (Book IV, Section ii: 12). Smith's famous message opens a chapter in the theory of international trade. Adopting Smith's labor theory of value, Ricardo formulates his principle of comparative advantage[60] in Chapter 7 of *Principle of Political Economy and Taxation* (1817). Ricardo's principle of comparative advantage is designed to deal with the trade between two nations: England and Portugal. In Ricardo's illustration, a nation is treated as a unit of analysis. However, instead of assuming, as Adam Smith did, that England is more productive in producing one good and Portugal in the other; Ricardo assumes that Portugal is more productive in both goods. As long as the internal (opportunity) cost ratios between both countries differ, Ricardo is able to show that specialization by each country in the goods in which it has a comparative advantage can increase aggregate world output using the same amount of labor. This principle is later incorporated into the supply-and-demand approach, through the Heckscher-Ohlin model.[61] For almost two centuries, the principle of comparative advantage has dominated the neoclassical theory of international trade. Today, mainstream neoclassical international economists continue to adopt Richardian methods in their analysis. For these scholars, the function of a global economy is conceived of a mechanism to be analyzed in strict isolation from any political, moral or sociological consideration. In other words, the operation of the laws of international trade should be independent of the moral belief of the human agent. Furthermore, in their view, causal relationships in the social and economic spheres can only be established by long-term tendencies due to the lack of exact measurement on its complexity (Pribram 1983: 169-171). Simply put, contemporary mainstream scholars, in the Classical – Ricardian traditions, are interested in investigating the long run equilibrium condition, adopting aggregate and static approaches in their international studies.

The purposes of this chapter are to identify the weaknesses in the mainstream neoclassical trade theory, and suggest a new direction of research agenda. Specifically, this chapter recommends to adopt the Schutzian theory of human agency (Weber 1947/1964; Schutz 1970: 1-50) in understanding international trade. Following Max Weber (1947/1964: 87-118), Schutz

[60] It has been claimed that Robert Torrens deserves the credit for discovering the law of comparative advantage in his *Essay on the External Corn Trade* (1815). Ruffin (2002: 727-748) argues that though Torrens pointed out that absolute advantage may not enable us to decide whether a good would be imported, 'his statement of comparative advantage was too incomplete for easy scientific reproducibility'.

[61] For a historical account of the development of the neoclassical theory of international trade, see Haberler (1961) and Gomes (1990).

(1970: 1-50) argues that action has meaning attached to it as human agents make sense of their everyday life. Making sense of the external world means interpretation. When human agents experience, their knowledge grows. This stock of knowledge serves as a scheme of interpretation and determines their anticipation of things to come. Individuals assess incoming events in the light of the difference between what has been expected and what has actually happened. When expectations differ from outcomes, this implies 'errors' and agents need to modify their actions. The process of re-interpretation constructs new meanings and at the same time reduces uncertainty. This Schutzian framework will be served as a critique to the neoclassical pure theory of international trade (see below). Hitherto, scholars in Austrian economics have extended their criticisms on many aspects of the mainstream neoclassical theories including methodology, development economics, monetary theory, public finance and comparative economic systems. Surprisingly, little has been said on the pure theory of international trade, though F.A. Hayek and L. von Mises contribute significantly to the international monetary theory in general and the debate of exchange rates systems in particular (Viser 1988: 107, 118).[62] This chapter attempts to fill this gap. It will argue that the human agency approach, if further applied, can contribute tremendously to many global issues such as international economic order and globalization.

6.2 Problems in mainstream neoclassical international trade theories

Though the labor theory of value has been generally abandoned by contemporary scholars in international economics and sophisticated quantitative and computer techniques are widely applied, the theories of international trade today still suffer from the major drawback of oversimplifying social world phenomena. In particular, the modern version of the Ricardian theory of international trade, in its most simple form, assumes two countries producing two commodities using labor as the only factor of production. Commodities are assumed homogeneous across firms and countries. Labor is homogeneous within a country but heterogeneous across countries. Commodities can be transported costless between countries. Labor can be reallocated costless between industries within a country but cannot move between countries. There is a full

[62] Austrian economists generally argue that international trade theory should not be separated from general trade theory. In Murray Rothbard's view, 'international trade' is just a practical example of the 'general theory of trade' (See Machaj 2004).

employment of labor. Production technology differs across industries and countries and are reflected in labor productivity. Under the assumption of perfect competition, firms maximize profit while consumers maximize utility. While scholars in social economics, evolutionary economics and Austrian economics have criticized the neoclassical theory of market exchange which adopts the concept of Paretian optimality, none of them focuses exclusively on the theory of international trade.[63] Gunning (2003) rightly notes, 'It seems evident that if economists took account of the implications of the praxeological approach to international trade, they would want to make major revisions in the fundamental theory. This, in turn, is likely to lead to fundamental revisions in the evaluation of arguments for and against free trade and in policy recommendations'. In the following section, some major problems of contemporary neoclassical theories of international trade are identified.

6.3 Trade between two countries versus trade between two individuals from different nations

In neoclassical international economics, a nation is taken as a basic unit of analysis. However, a nation, despite being created by its people, is never a human agent. To say that two nations trade, is merely a metaphor. It must not be taken to mean that a nation itself has any reality apart from the acts of individuals (Rothbard 1993: 2). A nation, which is socially constructed (see the previous section), becomes meaningful only through the actions of its people. For Max Weber (1947/1964), in social science, there is no such thing as a collective personality which 'acts'. Extending Weber's insights, when reference is made in an economic context to collectivities such as a nation, what is meant is only a certain kind of development of actual or possible social actions of the individual persons. On this, Rothbard (1973: 81) plainly adds that:

> 'only an individual has a mind; only an individual can feel, see, sense, and perceive; only an individual can act ... It implies that such collective concepts as groups, nations, and states do not actually

[63] This is evidenced by the fact that the discussion of the theory of international trade does not appear in Von Mises (1949) nor Rothbard (1993). Neither it is included in the basic Austrian economics textbooks such as Shand (1984) and Reekie (1984) nor in the three volumes of Austrian economics readings edited by Littlechild (1990). In a recent article, Gunning (2003) discusses the concept of praxeological entrepreneurship in the global economy.

exist or act; they are only metaphorical constructs for describing the similar or concerted actions of individuals'.

It may be argued that treating a nation as a unit of analysis is only a short-cut method in economic investigation. This method arguably allows economists to simplify the complexity of social world phenomena and thus can be defended as an expository expedient. However, using this short-cut aggregation approach, the neoclassical models lose insight of the market process in the world economy.[64]

We examine how a focus on human agency or the use of a 'first person perspective' (Addleson 1995) can influence the analysis of international trade. If we view international transactions from the trader's point of view, then the concept of comparative advantage may have little relevance in understanding human action because traders themselves do not even know the concept or the comparative cost ratios at all. Moreover, the principle of comparative advantage assumes a certain amount of factor endowments between two countries. It is important to point out that creative entrepreneurship can alter the given resource situation of an economy and hence its comparative advantage (Yu 1997: 159; 2003: 69). Therefore, Porter (1990: 65) is right to contend that 'the principle of comparative advantage ... fails to capture the determinants of economic success in the modern world economy'. Unlike the neoclassical approach which assumes a set of known alternatives and costs data for comparing the comparative advantage of producing various commodities of two nations, traders do not possess such information. Therefore we cannot expect merchants to compute the comparative cost ratios in international trade. Instead, in the global market, given genuine uncertainty, business people do economic calculation (Von Mises 1949) via trial and error, guided by profits. Starting with a business plan, they attempt to determine what orders are to be given, which factors are to be utilized, and how their resources will be used. They also need to predict future demand conditions by taking into account of the actions of competitors. Having made their determinations and predictions, they proceed to make judgements concerning the profitability of alternative plans. When they ultimately make the decision to trade, they are in effect betting on their judgements (Knight 1921). Therefore, the actual market process is much more complicated than those modeled by neoclassical international economists. On the other hand, our subjectivist approach allows us to interpret human actions in the world trade from the

[64] For a discussion of some shortcomings of economic aggregation, see Reekie (1984: 56-61).

first person point of view, and provides valuable and more realistic policy implications (see next section).

6.4 Comparative advantage and subjective cost: the beaver and deer revisited

In analyzing international trade, contemporary neoclassical scholars treat costs as objective and observable. Consider the original Adam Smith's beaver and deer example (Smith 1776/1937: 47):

> 'If among a nation of hunters ... it usually costs twice the labor to kill a beaver which it costs to kill a deer, one beaver should naturally exchange for or be worth two deer'.

Smith assumes that for *each* hunter, the resource input (i.e. homogeneous labor) of killing a beaver is twice the input of killing a deer, then the exchange rate in the market would be one beaver for two deer. While the resource outlays (observable costs) for killing an animal may be the same for each average hunter, the subjective cost of killing an animal for each hunter can never be the same. The total resource outlays may be observable and can be calculated objectively in an accounting system. However, the subjective cost of an option involves more than observable outlays. It involves psychic costs too. This subjective cost can only be mentally perceived and estimated by a human agent (Buchanan 1969). This value does not exist outside the human mind. Therefore, it cannot be calculated by an observer, economist or a policy maker. It follows that the principle of comparative advantage which bases on the calculation of objective costs has limited use in understanding international trade in particular and human agent's action in general.

Furthermore, when 'the first person approach' is introduced, the analysis of the trade between residents of two nations involves more than just a mechanical optimization exercise. Instead, international trade is an extremely complicated process involving subjective understanding of the actor's interpretation of the outside world. This subjective interpretation is, in turn, associated with actor's social and cultural backgrounds. Unfortunately, the neoclassical world consists merely of the unbounded antagonistic moves of independent actors. International merchants are the isolated units and that international relations are frictionless. Foreign trade in the neoclassical paradigm is composed of merchants independent and mindless of each other, or if strategically aware of competitors, this awareness is understood to be unwilling to alter competitive outcomes. Hence, the neoclassical modeling of international trade is 'transhistoric and acultural' (Abolafia and Biggart 1992: 316-317). In recent decades, using the concepts of transaction costs and opportunism, new institutionalists begin to deal with trust and culture in international trade. In particular, Greif (1994) examines the employment of agents to extend trade into distant markets and shows how low-trust 'individualists' could be more successful at exporting their trading system than high-trust 'collectivists'. He explains why the 17th century Genoese has greater internationalizing success over Maghribi traders. Members of both regions are assumed to form their expectations of potential trading strategies on the basis of their closeness to the group they knew, and likelihood of sharing its 'cultural beliefs'. The Genoese merchants, who refuse to share information about which agents they can trust, have to pay those agents more to stop them cheating. However, this additional cost of intra group trade is offset by the saving from not joining the information network; and individualists' greater willingness to hire unknown agents at a premium over known and trustworthy agents gives them a greater incentive to reap the extra trade gains made available by voyages of discovery. Greif (1994: 931) concludes that 'Individualist cultural beliefs lead to an 'integrated' society in which inter-economy agency relations are established because they are efficient. Collectivist cultural beliefs create a wedge between efficient and profitable agency relations, leading to a 'segregated' society in which efficient inter-economy agency relations are not established'. Despite Greif's excellent historical research and insights, his emphasis on opportunistic behavior (cheating) in international trade costs him insight on coordination problems. Using mathematical models to incorporate opportunistic or holdup behaviors, new institutional contributions are increasingly integrated into the mainstream neoclassical paradigm.

6.5 Non-entrepreneurial trading system: static uncertainty and non-creativeness

While the orthodox neoclassical approach using aggregate production function in development economics has long been criticized, the same approach to economics of international trade has suffered less criticisms.[65] Similar to the theory of economic growth, neoclassical assumptions of rational human conduct, frictionless decision-making and profit maximization have made the theory of international trade distant away from the reality. The conventional neoclassical approach to the world trade 'fails to address uncertainty, bounded rationality ... institutional complexity or the dynamics of actual adjustment processes' (Nelson and Winter 1982: 5). International trade in the neoclassical paradigm is simply an exercise of choosing among known alternatives. Manufacturers or merchants in the global economy are then assumed to employ mathematical or optimization techniques to reach a decision. In the neoclassical international trade model, there is no room for enterprise or initiative, clever strategies, ingenious schemes, brilliant innovations, or charisma and more seriously, no need for mutual information among individual participants in the market process (Baumol 1968: 68; Leibenstein 1968: 72; Kirzner 1985: 16). In essence, the aggregate approach in the mainstream trade models ignores genuine uncertainty, knowledge and dynamic learning. Accordingly, nothing can be discovered regarding new ways of using given resources or regarding the existence of hitherto unnoticed resources. As Gunning (2003) rightly argues, the principle of comparative advantage assumes:

> 'only limited scope for imagination, creativity and inventiveness. In making their calculations, the agents are assumed to have only limited interaction. At some point, each is assumed to find out that his opportunity cost differs from that faced by the other and, therefore, that there are potential gains from trade ... However, humans have the ability to at least partly infer, from the consequence of another person's action, the sequence of steps that preceded the consequences. A human being can even partly infer the mental processes that the other person uses to decide what action to take'.

Hence, Gunning highlights the significance of intersubjectivity in human action. In short, when imagination, creativity and inventiveness are incorporated economic analysis of international trade, many neoclassical arguments will become invalid.

65 Cheung (1987: 129) comments that the fate of the two major theories developed in the 1950s, namely economic development and international trade are different. While the theory of economic growth is largely abandoned due to its absurdity, the theory of international trade gains high respects among the economists.

6.6 A new direction in international trade theory: a human agency approach

An alternative to the mainstream neoclassical paradigm is the human agency framework advanced by Austrian/German scholars such as A. Schutz, M. Weber, L. Von Mises and F. Hayek.[66] This approach to economics of international trade involves human agent's interpretation, learning, experimentation and entrepreneurial discovery on the one hand, and a broader social construction on the other.[67]

6.7 To trade or not to trade, it is a subjective interpretation problem

To understand international trade is to understand human actions in the world economy. Understanding an international trade action is to investigate how the human agent interprets oncoming events from the external world. At previously mentioned, human agents find at any given point of time an interpretation framework or a stock of knowledge at hand that serves them as a scheme of interpretation of their past and present experiences, and also determines their anticipation of things to come. This stock of knowledge or a subjective interpretative framework is derived from actors' everyday life experiences and has a history. In other words, knowledge and experiences are socially constructed and taken for granted by the actor. In the world of genuine uncertainty, human agents attempt to cope with the external world by constructing, in their minds, templates of features of the world and then seeing whether or not these templates actually fit (Earl 1983: 140). Correct interpretation of other market participant's actions means better coordination, which also implies economizing. Conversely, incorrect interpretation means coordination failure and results in what the neoclassical international economists refer to as 'an inefficient use of resources'.

Since actors' knowledge is derived from experiences and biographically determined, accordingly, actor's interpretation of the external world is bounded by his/her cultures and social backgrounds. Hence, our human

[66] For some historical accounts of integration of Schutz's subjectivist approach into Austrian economics, see Prendergast (1986), Pietrykowski (1996) and Koppl (1997).

[67] For an account of the method of Austrian subjectivism, see O'Driscoll and Rizzo (1985); Yu (1999; 2001a).

agency approach is consistent with the socio-economic approach[68] which views international issues from a cultural perspective (for example, see Berger 1991; Biggart and Orru 1997; Whitley 1999). Following scholars in Austrian and social economics, we argue that action is oriented towards others, has underlying norms, and is sustained by institutional arrangements (Abolafia and Biggart 1992: 315). Global market participants are socially oriented and have intersubjective orientations: they recognize each other as contestants and observe each other closely. International exchange is understood as social action structured by political, economic and cultural context. Therefore, world markets are social arenas that structure exchange and competition according to legitimated organising principles. As Granovetter (1985: 487) notes, 'actors do not behave or decide as atoms outside a social context ... Their attempts at purposive action are instead embedded in concrete, ongoing systems of social relations'. Applying the socio-economic insight, the international trade process is thus understood as actions structured by a specific political, economic and cultural context.

6.8 Dynamic learning, experimentation and error elimination

The contemporary neoclassical trade models do not rule out the effect of learning (for example, see Boldrin and Scheinkman 1988; Scherer 1996; Young 1991). However, learning in the neoclassical paradigm is static in nature, involving nothing more than an optimization of various *known* options. Dynamic or entrepreneurial learning is 'more than mathematical computation, rather it consists of the setting up of the problem situation itself or the movement from one problem situation to another' (O'Driscoll and Rizzo 1985: 37). It takes place when the agent's framework of interpreting external messages of stimuli has changed over time.

Human agents in the global market learn by trial and error, a measure adopted by most organisms. Karl Popper (1972: 242) argues 'all organisms are constantly engaging in problem solving which "always" proceeds by the method of trial and error; new reactions, new forms, new organs, new modes of behavior, new hypothesis, are tentatively put forward and controlled by error-elimination'. Agreeing with Popper, Hayek argues that the market is an ongoing, open-ended process of trial and error, a process

[68] For an account of the socio-economic approach, see Etzioni and Lawrence (1991).

in which constantly a number of potential alternative solutions of various kinds of problems are tried out and selected upon through the choices of market participants. It is a process in which new tentative problem-solutions are continuously explored, and in which the problems themselves are subject to change, as solutions to old problems tend to create new problems. The learning process involves the history of the actor's own experience of success and failure. Agents interpret or classify incoming events according to their own experience. Whenever expectations resulting from the existing interpretation are disappointed, or when beliefs so far held are disproved by new experience, then re-interpretation or reclassification occurs. The whole process of dynamic learning, of the growth of knowledge, is then seen as consisting of such re-interpretation or re-classification, as a process in which our 'frame of reference' is corrected, adjusted, or refined (Vanberg 1993: 97).

Further insights on the learning process can be gained by applying Harper's (1996) growth of knowledge theory. Merchants in the world market are constantly engaged in solving problems which tend to involve much novelty and which are ill-specified (Harper 1994: 56). Whenever actual events diverge from their predictions, traders learn that something is wrong with their stock of knowledge. They know that they cannot hold on to their existing conjectural framework (Harper 1994: 63). Simply put, the failure of a plan must be due to inadequate knowledge of the circumstances in which the action has to be taken. Previously unsuccessful policies prompt the need for a revision of trading plans. A new array of plans is formed, each with a tentative solution to the original problem. The number or variety of solutions proposed is limited by the trader's creativity and imagination (Harper 1994: 71). The new plan too is problematic. Each trial solution is controlled by a process of attempted error-elimination. Error elimination is done through the testing of ideas in practice, which involves the comparison and assessment of rival conjectures in terms of how well they can solve the problems (Harper 1994: 72). In this way, a change in trading plan can be viewed as a result of a mutual adjustment process of continuous interpretations of external information and plan revisions among all agents in the world economy.

6.9 Entrepreneurial discovery

Due to diverse experiences, human agents respond differently to the same objectively defined stimulus (O'Driscoll and Rizzo 1985: 38-39; Yu 1999).

In simple terms, the cognitive patterns are asymmetrical. The lack of symmetry gives rise to creativity and novelty (DeBono 1992: 15). Hence, our theory of human agency sheds light on entrepreneurial innovation and discovery in the global arena. Entrepreneurial innovation is a dynamic learning process. International merchants or business people are not passive robots. They do not only adapt themselves to the external world but also adjust the environment to their needs through deliberate and conscious choices. Besides being diffusers and uses of knowledge, these agents are also a source of knowledge. In other words, they are builders and users of knowledge, creators of economic processes and above all, the engine of change (Hayek 1952; see also Rizzello 1999). Human agents around the world constantly create reasons for their own existence, trying to influence as much as possible and to determine as much as possible the future states of the world in a direction that favors their own development (Rizzello 2000: 127-150). In the global market, when agents can see things differently and are able to move out of the routine track and create, then they can be regarded as entrepreneurs. Modifying the categories of their framework (Lane *et al.* 1996), or in some cases even adding a new category, these entrepreneurial agents are able to give others a different sense of the meaning through re-creation. Creative activity thus involves the shifting of all different sets of reference frames that would usually be ordered differently and be seen as incompatible – until something clicks into place as a new way of looking at how things fit together. Such discovery means that the entrepreneurial agent is able to escape from the existing patterns of interpretation and reorganizes ideas into new sequences (DeBono 1992: 15). The international entrepreneur always 'embodies the possibilities of escape from what might otherwise appear to us to be incomprehensible, or from what might otherwise appear to us to be a chaotic, indifferent, or incorrigible world' (Thayer 1988: 250, 254).

6.10 International trade, knowledge transmission and the market process

In the neoclassical international trade paradigm, knowledge is either given or totally ignored. If economics is a coordination problem (Hayek 1945), then it is of utmost importance to analyze how knowledge is created and transmitted during the process of international exchange. Assuming two persons A and B living in England and Portugal respectively, each possesses their own stock of knowledge and do subjective interpretation on oncoming events each day. A wishes to attend end X and B, end Y.

Each of them attempts to do economic assessment and makes judgement regards to their external environments. A would like to achieve his end but he does not have the mean at his disposal. Furthermore, he does not know where and how to obtain such a mean. On the other hand, B owes abundant resource/mean which she has no use for her purpose, though the resource is suitable for A to attain his end. The economic problem is that A and B do not know each other. Obviously, in this case, international trade cannot be carried out for both lacking of knowledge. According to the subjectivist theory of knowledge (Kirzner 1979: 137-153), to these two parties, the opportunity for them simply does not exist.[69]

Even if merchants of the two nations accidentally discover that both of them have the intention to trade, the international transaction may not be carried out for both parties' actions are socially embedded. Traders' minds are governed by a set of habits, traditions, institutions, norms, customs and legal rules which make them follow without being asked. This knowledge is taken for granted and is socially constructed. Each trading party, with different cultures and values, will accordingly interpret the social world differently. Specifically, it takes lots of efforts to find out if the trading partner is trustworthy. This can be illustrated by the first time trade between English and Chinese during the late Ch'ing Dynasty. Their trade encounter unfortunately ended with a conflict, the Opium War. The cultural content of the Sino-British conflict can be seen by the fact that British referred to this war as a 'trade war'. For the British, the purpose of the war was to demand a free trade with China and eliminate unfair treatment laid down by the Ch'ing government officials. However, the Chinese referred the conflict to as an 'Opium War' because of enormous amount of opium shipped to China, leading to moral degradation and loss of foreign exchange (silver).[70] Hence, knowing your trading parties, making entrepreneurial move, learning and testing foreign markets by trials and errors are the main elements in international trade. However, such important elements are missing in the neoclassical paradigm.

The issue of culture and knowledge makes justification for the role of middleman in international trade. To be sure, the role of middleman is well documented in the mainstream price and transaction costs theories

[69] The subjectivist approach does not stress knowledge itself, but rather what people know about knowledge. This approach focuses on the kind of knowledge about which people know nothing at all. It follows that 'things about which men are completely ignorant are things that simply do not exist' (Kirzner 1979: 138). See also Yu (2001a: 47-63).

[70] For a further discussion of the Sino-British conflict, see Yu (2003: 76-78).

(for example, see Casson 1982; Reekie 1984). However, in our human agency perspective, a middleman is more than just a person who links both parties together. The middleman, in our case, is also an entrepreneur as well as a knowledge creator. He or she transmits knowledge and performs entrepreneurial discovery, and hence, raises the well being of both trading parties.

In the above example, assume persons A and B do things routinely each day, and a third person C practices as a middleman.[71] C discovers that there is an opportunity in the international market. He contacts B and offers to buy the resource which B has abundance and sells it to A. As a consequence of C's entrepreneurial action, all three parties gain. This is essentially the case of Kirznerian entrepreneurship (Kirzner 1973) which conducts arbitrageurship.[72] The neoclassical analysis would argue that the trade would continue until marginal rate of substitutions between two goods for all parties equal. Their analysis would end at the optimal equilibrium. Unfortunately, such technical analysis, though elegantly presented, loses the insight of how agents behave and how knowledge is created and transmitted. According to De Soto (1995: 234-237), there are at least three significant implications due to the result of entrepreneurial arbritageurship.

Firstly, by performing as a middleman, entrepreneur C has created new information which does not exist before. An entrepreneurial act implies a creation of information which takes place in the agent's mind. In our case, information is created by C. Moreover, as soon as C enters into the transaction with A and B, new information is also created in the minds of A and B. As a result of C's action, A becomes aware that the resource that he lacks is available in another part of the world. Hence, A would take a new action that he does not consider before. On the other hand, B also becomes aware that the abundant resource she possesses can now be sold overseas at a good price too. Therefore, B also takes a new action previously not taken before. In short, C's entrepreneurial action gives rise to a chain of new knowledge in the world market.

Secondly, the entrepreneurial creation of knowledge implies a simultaneous transmission of knowledge in the global market. Knowledge transmission

[71] Adopted from De Soto (1995: 228-253). Using simple stickmen as an illustration, De Soto is able to demonstrate the essence of Austrian entrepreneurial process.

[72] White (1976: 4) argues that Kirzner does not distinguish arbitrageurship from entrepreneurship.

means that people learn from others and create new knowledge in their minds as a result of learning. In our example, new ideas have been created in the minds of A and B respectively at the same time as a result of C's entrepreneurial action: (1) Trader A now may proceed to pursue his desired goal which could not be attended due to lack of specific kind of resource owned by B. (2) Trader B now realizes that her resource is useful and valuable, and therefore should not be wasted. It can be conceived that in general, through the prices signal, such knowledge (received by both A and B) will be spread to the entire global community in the market process.

Thirdly, through learning, trading parties revise their plans, formulate new expectation (Lachmann 1956) and make economic judgement (Knight 1921) to the new situation. Hence, economizing resources or more precisely, coordination of actors' subjective interpretation will be possible. In our case, as a result of C's entrepreneurial action, both A and B would revise their plans in accordance to the new messages they perceive. In particular, person A, now having the resource at his disposal, can attend his end and undertake action that he did not take previously. On the other hand, person B does not waste her resource any more, but keeps and conserves it in order to sell it in the international market. Therefore, all trading parties in the market will learn, revise their plans, and modify their actions accordingly, thereby economic coordination is made possible. More importantly, each party adjusts to the world market in the best possible way without knowing that they are actually learning. As Schutz and Luckmann (1989: 8) note, 'one learns both to "adjust" one's own conduct appropriately to the goal of action and also to improve one's interpretation of the conduct of others'. This interactive market process, a simple and effective way of coordinating economic activities and improving human welfare, is precisely Adam Smith's concept of invisible hand.

In summary, our illustration reiterates the argument that knowledge in the global market is never objective. Instead, it is always subjective and only exists in the minds of traders who are capable of perceiving, discovering, creating and interpreting it. Hence, knowledge and ignorance governs the analysis of the international trade.

6.11 Further implications

This chapter has argued that mainstream neoclassical theories of international trade are mechanistic, acultural, ahistorical and non-entrepreneurial. It has suggested a new direction in research in international trade: the Schutzian theory of human agency. If the Austrian subjectivist approach is applied to other aspects of international economics, it will shed new lights on many global issues. The followings are some examples.

6.11.1 The role of global entrepreneurship and internationalization

Our emphasis on human agency approach in international trade highlights the important role of entrepreneurship in the globalization. As mentioned, human agents are not passive robots. Besides being diffusers and users of knowledge, they are also a source of knowledge and the engine of change. In the international market, some agents behave as Schumpeterian entrepreneurs.[73] Their extraordinary discovery radically change the way of doing things (for example, Bill Gates' IT revolution). Other agents behave as adaptive entrepreneurs. Their ordinary discoveries help to refine and perfect the technology advanced by Schumpeterian entrepreneurs. Assume that initially an extraordinary discovery occurs in an economically advanced nation. In other words, Schumpeterian entrepreneurs perceive that it is possible to pursue their interests more effectively than they have done so far. Consequently, other market participants (both foreign and domestic) find that their stocks of knowledge are no longer adequate to interpret the newly emerging events. Their interpretative frameworks are incapable of coordinating economic activities because the meanings attached to them have changed significantly. Technological breakthrough brought about by Schumpeterian entrepreneur does not only create confusion in the global market but also profit opportunities to other business people. Given new technologies, new relative prices and tastes, adaptive entrepreneurs all over the world soon identify these new opportunities. They try to capitalize on these opportunities by refining production methods, modifying and improving models (Cheah 1994). At the beginning, there may be few imitators but later the number increases. Moreover, under keen competition, imitators modify their production or transaction methods with the aim of improving profit margins. Gradually, successful practices spread all over the world and become a rule of thumb or routine in the international business operation. Hence, global businesses such as retail franchises (for example, 7-Eleven) or original equipment manufacturer (OEM)[74] emerge. The process of internalization

[73] For a review of Schumpeterian and adaptive of entrepreneurship, see Yu (1997).

[74] For a discussion of OEM, see Yu (1997).

involves interactions of millions of entrepreneurs' constantly interpreting their environments. It is also the consequence of interactions between exploration and exploitation in entrepreneurial learning.

6.11.2 Understanding the nature of 'free trade and protectionism'

The issue of free trade has long been a hot debate among politicians and economists. This is especially true when the world economy is at present experiencing rapid globalization due to the revolution in information technology. Most contemporary neoclassical economists, using Paretian efficiency concept, hold the view that free trade will be benefiting to all trading nations. Trade restrictions are often seen by them as a result of rent seeking activities articulated by interest groups such as exporters or manufacturers and therefore regarded as unproductive (for example, see Tullock 1967).

In our human agency perspective, trades are never 'free'. Instead, agents' actions are governed by their knowledge and experiences. Each trade decision involves actor's subjective interpretation of foreign and domestic conditions. Interpretations are socially embedded and associated with culture, customs, norms and social expectations, etc. Before international transactions are realized, trading agents, based on their experience and knowledge, will first assess their foreign partners. This includes whether their trading partners are trustworthy, share the same culture, or sympathetic with their religious belief, etc. (for example, Muslims would be hostile to American firms). Obviously, people are more prone to trade with people who share common culture or belief. In a sense, all international trades have moral contexts. Therefore, international trades are never free and have moral standard too; it is thus not surprised to find that the transaction of narcotics is generally forbidden. Too greedy in trade is regarded as immoral. For example, giant multi-corporation sport manufacturers are often being condemned for exploiting cheap labor in developing nations. Fast food chain stores such as McDonald's or KFC are being attacked by the anti-globalization groups because these multinational corporations are blamed for widening the income gaps between rich and poor nations.

The culture of a country is often reflected in government policies conducted by the state. International trade differs from domestic trade in that it involves national sovereignty. The formation of a nation state is the result of a long-term evolution of the coordinating actions of its people. People within a nation share the same social identity. A state is socially constructed.[75] The legitimacy of the national government originates from its people taking knowledge and experience for granted. Just like children unquestioningly accepting their father and mother as their parents, people accept their government as their national protector or leader. In this sense, theories of rent seeking or lobbying the government by interest groups in Public Choice School tell only part of the story. Rent seeking activities such as tariff or import quota (which are unproductive as regarded by neoclassical public choice school) arise only partly due to rent seekers. Instead, they arise mainly as a result of our construction of social reality that a government is supposed to protect the interests of its citizens. We are willing to pay taxes to the government in exchange for the government to provide us protective services or fight externally for our interests. This constructed relationship arises out of the spontaneous order. Hence, our argument reiterates the concept of public interest in political science which is largely rejected by public choice school scholars.

If we accept the argument that a national government is socially constructed and its function is to serve the public interest of its citizens, then our human agency perspective can shed light on the nature of international protectionism. So far, most arguments against trade barriers are ideological. Our theory of social reality suggests that complete free trades will happen only if all people are in the same nation. As long as trades involve *national* border crossing, trades would never be free. Hence, the solution to eliminate trade barriers, in terms of the human agency approach, is to integrate nations together as one. For example, within European Union (EU), free mobility of labor and resources are possible for member countries for members consider themselves as one nation. Trades between Australia and New Zealand involve fewer restrictions due to the fact that both countries have their European origins and cultures of the two nations are very much alike. Based on this, my suggestion is bold, if not provocative. Efforts should be made to merge all nations to one single global community. When there is no national difference, trades will be much freer. In other words, after national sovereignties and borders are abolished, trade barriers and protections will be greatly reduced. Of course, by that time, some trade barriers still remain due to cultural, religious and ethnic differences. However, such influences can be reduced slowly over time through the education of the idea of one globe, or in our theory, the social construction of one community.

[75] The new institutional school argues that a state is formed to reduce transaction costs through the evolution of property rights (see North 1990).

6.11.3 International Monetary Fund (IMF) as a coordination institution in the evolving global economy

As mentioned, human agents interpret external events based on their stock of knowledge accumulated from everyday life. Therefore, each individual interprets differently on an external event. As a result, there are diverse expectations for the future economic condition in the market. With genuine uncertainty, wrong expectations (or economic errors) in the market contribute to a business cycle. In the extreme case, systematic errors committed by the general public lead to periodical economic chaos and thus, severe business fluctuation. By that time, market participants' stocks of knowledge are incapable to interpret correctly external events. Hence, economic coordination fails. If the failure is widespread, it may lead to international economic disasters such as the Great Depression in the 1930s. Human agents do learn from experiences. They know that a better understanding and cooperation among people of different nations and national governments can reduce the risk of coordination failure. By trial and error, and experimentation, international agents such as the International Monetary Fund (IMF), World Trade Organization (WTO) and World Bank, have been established to help to do economic coordination.

The basic objective of the IMF, in my view, is to put the world economy into a common understanding framework.[76] As mentioned, economic chaos is the result of coordination failure. The basic solution to the coordination failure is to increase the understanding of other person's actions and thus increase the chances of success in coordination. This can be done by setting up a formal international organization called the IMF. The purpose of the IMF is to provide a set of rules which generally lay down clear lines of authority and communication with the intention of ensuring that the IMF goal may be attained (Silverman 1970: 14). By asking the Fund members to subordinate their in-order-to motives to the officially defined goals, the organization attempts de facto to substitute an objective context of meaning for the subjective configuration in which the individual member discovers the meaning of its action (Jehenson 1973: 227). The world taken for granted inside the IMF is thus composed of member countries following typical courses of action prompted by a

[76] According to Stanley Fischer *et al.* (2003: 45), the functions of the IMF are: (1) undertaking surveillance of the global economy and the economies of its members; (2) providing technical assistance to its members; (3) providing the machinery for consultation and collaboration on international monetary problems and (4) lending to its member countries.

set of invariant, typical motives. In other words, member countries are given expectations about appropriate acts for themselves and others when in various status positions. As a result, they are then able to apprehend the meanings associated with the economic actions of other people and to form a view of self based on the responses of others. Members will meet the expectations of others because these expectations are part of the definitions of themselves (i.e. they have been internalized). In essence, IMF members conform to a set of shared values which is central to the existence of a stable environment (Silverman 1970: 131). In this way, the IMF creates a 'communicative common environment' (Schutz 1970: 31, 165). It is a situational environment shared by all members who are able to communicate with one another. By establishing this international organization, the IMF is in fact building a coherent world of knowledge[77] and a cultural community (Schutz 1970: 81). Grouping members under 'one roof' (common environment), IMF facilitates mutual understanding and consent among countries. However, in recent years, the IMF seems to fail performing this important coordination function. In particular, the IMF is recently charged with lacking leadership in tackling the current Financial Tsunami. The failure can be originated from two sources. On the one hand, with rapid development of information technology, new financial instruments keep emerging that IMF and government organizations have difficult to keep pace with. Without updated technical and practical knowledge on market operations, IMF officials are unable to monitor members' activities and coordinate global financial affairs. On the other hand, the IMF is a huge international organization strongly embedded with rules and institutions, it cannot avoid to suffer from organizational inertia.[78] Given structural rigidity within the organization, IMF officials are slow to respond to the rapidly changing world. This chapter suggests that recommendations to the IMF reform should be made with human agency as the centre of analysis.

References

Abolafia, M. and N. Biggart (1992) Competitive Systems: A Sociological View. In: P. Ekins and M. Max-Neef (eds.) *Real-Life Economics: Understanding Wealth Creation.* London, UK: Routledge, pp. 315-23.

[77] Schutz (1970: 80) argues that the world of knowledge is incoherent, only partially clear and not free from contradiction.

[78] For a subjectivist explanation of institutional change and organizational inertia, see Yu (2001b: 217-236).

Addleson, M. (1995) *Equilibrium versus Understanding.* London, UK: Routledge.

Baumol, W.J. (1968) Entrepreneurship in Economic Theory. *American Economic Review Papers and Proceedings,* vol. 58, 64-71.

Berger, B. (1991) *The Culture of Modern Entrepreneurship.* San Francisco, USA: ICS Press.

Biggart, N.W. and M. Orru (1997) Societal Strategic Advantage: Automotive and Electronics Industries in East Asia. In: A. Bugru and B. Usdiken (eds.) *State, Market and Organizational Forms.* Berlin, Germany: de Gruyer, pp. 201-239.

Boldrin, M. and J. Scheinkman (1988) Learning-By-Doing, International Trade and Growth: A Note. UCLA Economics Working Papers, No 462.

Buchanan, J.M. (1969) *Cost and Choice: An Inquiry in Economic Theory.* Chicago, USA: Markham Publishing Co.

Casson, M. (1982) *The Entrepreneur: An Economic Theory.* Oxford, UK: Blackwell.

Cheah, H.B. (1994) Creativity in the Entrepreneurial Process. In: S. Dingli (ed.) *Creative Thinking: A Multifaceted Approach.* Msida, Malta: Malta University Press.

Cheung, S.N.S. (1987) *Further Comments on China.* Hong Kong, China PR: Shun Po [text in Chinese].

De Soto, J.H. (1995) Entrepreneurship and the Economic Analysis of Socialism. In: G. Meijer (ed.) *New Perspectives on Austrian Economics.* London, UK: Routledge, pp. 228-253.

DeBono, E. (1992) *Serious Creativity.* New York, USA: Harper Business.

Earl, P.E. (1983) *The Economic Imagination: Towards a Behavourial Analysis of Choice.* New York, USA: Sharpe Inc.

Etzioni, A. and P.R. Lawrence (eds.) (1991) *Socio-Economics: Towards a New Synthesis.* London, UK: M.E. Sharpe.

Fischer, S., A.H. Meltzer, J.D. Sachs and N. Stern (2003) The Future of the IMF and World Bank: Panel Discussion. *American Economics Review: Papers and Proceedings,* vol. 93 (2), 45-50.

Gomes, L. (1990) *Neoclassical International Economics: A Historical Survey.* New York, USA: St. Martin Press.

Granovetter, M. (1985) Economic Action and Social Structure: The Problem of Embeddedness. *The American Journal of Sociology,* vol. 91, 481-510.

Greif, A. (1994) Cultural Beliefs and the Organisation of Society. *Journal of Political Economy,* vol. 102 (5), 912-950.

Gunning, P. (2003) The Praxeological Concept of International Entrepreneurship. Working paper, available at: http://fortunecity.com/meltingpot/barclay/212/subjecti/workpape/intrnaent.htm.

Haberler, G. (1961) *A Survey of International Trade Theory.* In: A.Y.C. Koo (ed.) *Selected Essays of Gottfried Haberler.* Cambridge, USA: The MIT Press, pp. 55-108.

Harper, D.A. (1994) A New Approach to Modelling Endogenous Learning Processes In Economic Theory. In: P. Boettke, I. Kirzner and M. Rizzo (eds.) *Advances in Austrian Economics I.* Greenwich, USA: JAI Press.

Harper, D.A. (1996) *Entrepreneurship and the Market Process: An Enquiry into the Growth of Knowledge.* London, UK: Routledge.

Hayek, F.A. (1945) The Use of Knowledge in the Society. *American Economic Review,* vol. 35, 519-530.

Hayek, F.A. (1952) *The Sensory Order.* Chicago, USA: University of Chicago Press.

Jehenson, R. (1973) A Phenomenological Approach to the Study of the Formal Organisation. In: G. Psathas (ed.) *Phenomenological Sociology Issues and Applications.* New York, USA: John Wiley, pp. 219-47.

Kirzner, I. M. (1973) *Competition and Entrepreneurship.* Chicago, USA: University of Chicago Press.

Kirzner, I.M. (1979) *Perception, Opportunity and Profit.* Chicago, USA: University of Chicago Press.

Kirzner, I. M. (1985) *Discovery and the Capitalist Process.* Chicago, USA: University of Chicago press.

Knight, F. (1921) *Risk, Uncertainty and Profit.* Boston, USA: Houghton Fifflin.

Koppl, R. (1997) Mises and Schutz on Ideal Types. *Cultural Dynamics,* vol. 9 (1), 67-76.

Lachmann, L.M. (1956) *Capital and its Structure.* Kansas City, USA: Sheed Andrews and McMeel, Inc.

Lane, D., F. Malerba, R. Maxfield and L. Orsenigo (1996) Choice and Action. *Journal of Evolutionary Economics,* vol. 6, 43-76.

Leibenstein, H. (1968) Entrepreneurship and Development. *American Economic Review,* vol. 58, 72-83.

Littlechild, S. (1990) *Austrian Economics.* Aldershot, UK: Edward Elgar.

Machaj, M. (2004) Is There a Distinct Theory of International Trade? Daily Article posted on 19 January 2004, Auburn, USA: Ludwig von Mises Institute.

Nelson, R.R. and S.G Winter (1982) *An Evolutionary Theory of Economic Change.* Cambridge, USA: Harvard University Press.

North, D. (1990) *Institutions, Institutional Change and Economic Performance.* Cambridge, UK: Cambridge University Press.

O'Driscoll Jr., G.P. and M. Rizzo (1985) *The Economics of Time and Ignorance.* Oxford, UK: Blackwell.

Pietrykowski, B. (1996) Alfred Schutz and the Economists. *History of Political Economy,* vol. 28 (Summer), 219-244.

Popper, K. (1972) *Objective Knowledge: An Evolutionary Approach.* Oxford, UK: Oxford University Press.

Porter, M.E. (1990) *The Competitive Advantage of Nations.* New York, USA: The Free Press.

Prendergast, C. (1986) Alfred Schutz and the Austrian School of Economics. *American Journal of Sociology,* vol. 92 (1), 1-26.
Pribram, K. (1983) *A History of Economic Reasoning.* Baltimore, USA: John Hopkins University Press.
Reekie, W.D. (1984) *Markets, Entrepreneurs and Liberty: An Austrian View of Capitalism.* Brighton, UK: Wheatsheaf Books.
Rizzello, S. (1999) *The Economics of the Mind.* Aldershot, UK: Edward Elgar.
Rizzello, S. (2000) Economic Change, Subjective Perception, and Institutional Evolution. *Metroeconomica,* vol. 51 (2), 127-150.
Rothbard, M.N. (1973) *For a New Liberty,* rev. edition. New York, USA: Libertarian Review Foundation.
Rothbard, M.N. (1993) *Man, Economy and State,* Auburn, USA: Ludwig von Mises Institute.
Ruffin, R.J. (2002) David Ricardo's Discovery of Comparative Advantage. *History of Political Economy,* vol. 34 (winter), 727-748.
Scherer, F.M. (1996) Learning by Doing and International Trade in Semiconductors. In: E. Helmstadter and M. Perlman (eds.) *Behavioral Norms, Technological Progress, and Economic Dynamics.* Ann Arbor, USA: University of Michigan Press, pp. 247-260.
Schutz, A. (1970) *On Phenomenology and Social Relations.* Chicago, USA: The University of Chicago Press.
Schutz, A. and T. Luckmann (1989) *The Structures of the Life World.* Evanston, USA: Northwestern University Press, Vol.II.
Shand, A.H. (1984) *The Capitalist Alternative: An Introduction to Neo-Austrian Economics.* New York, USA: New York University Press.
Silverman, D. (1970) *The Theory of Organisations* London, UK: Heinemann.
Smith, A. (1776/1937) *The Wealth of Nations.* New York, USA: Random House, Modern Library edition.
Thayer, L. (1988) Leadership/communication: A Critical Review and a Modest Proposal. In: G.M. Goldhaber and G.A. Barnett (eds.) *Handbook of Organisational Communication,* Northwood, USA: Ablex, pp. 231-263.
Tullock, G. (1967) The welfare costs of tariffs, monopoly and theft. *Western Economic Journal,* vol. 5 (June), 224-232.
Vanberg, J.V. (1993) Rational choice, Rule-Following and Institutions: An Evolutionary Perspective. In: U. Maki, B. Gustafsson and C. Knudsen (eds.), *Rationality, Institutions and Economic Methodology.* London, UK: Routledge, pp. 171-200.
Viser, H. (1988) Austrian Thinking on International Economics. *Journal of Economic Studies,* vol. 15 (3/4), 106-122.
Von Mises, L. (1949) *Human Action,* 3rd edition. Chicago, USA: Contemporary Books Inc.

Weber, M. (1947/1964) *The Theory of Social and Economic Organisation.* New York, USA: The Free Press.
White, L.H. (1976) Entrepreneurship, Imagination and the Question of Equilibrium. In: S. Littlechild (ed.), *Austrian Economics,* Vol. III. Aldershot, UK: Edward Elgar, pp. 87-104.
Whitley, R. (1999) *Divergent Capitalisms.* Oxford, UK: Oxford University Press.
Young, Alwyn (1991) Learning by Doing and the Dynamic Effects of International Trade. *The Quarterly Journal of Economics,* vol. 106 (2), 369-405.
Yu, T.F-L. (1997) *Entrepreneurship and Economic Development in Hong Kong.* London, UK: Routledge.
Yu, T.F-L. (1999) Toward a Praxeological Theory of the Firm. *Review of Austrian Economics,* vol. 12 (1), 25-41.
Yu, T.F-L. (2001a) Entrepreneurial Alertness and Discovery. *Review of Austrian Economics,* vol. 14 (1), 47-63.
Yu, T.F-L. (2001b) An Entrepreneurial Perspective of Institutional Change. *Constitutional Political Economy,* vol. 12 (3), 217-236.
Yu, T.F-L. (2003) *East Asian Business Systems in the Evolutionary Perspective: Entrepreneurship and Coordination.* New York, USA: Nova Science.

Chapter 7.
Government as a learner

7.1 Introduction

It is generally known that the neoclassical economic analysis of the government behavior and policy is largely conducted in terms of perfect competition, static uncertainty and Pareto optimality. In mainstream public economics, the government is portrayed as an omnipotent agent who chooses among known alternatives. It never suffers from knowledge problems, nor does it make errors. It never needs to learn new things or revise plans, for all alternatives are known and can be attained costlessly. This situation remains until the re-discovery[79] of Coase's contributions. From Coase (1937, 1960), economists understand that inefficiencies in the market economy are due largely to transaction costs and that the so-called public goods and externality problems in fact arise from poorly defined property rights. The high costs of defining, metering and enforcing property rights lead to market failures (Cheung 1983). Coase's arguments have significant theoretical implications for the choice of economic institutions (Cheung 1989). Because of the existence of transaction costs, the socialist system is not necessarily superior to the capitalist system, or vice versa. Coase's contributions, which laid the foundation of the New Institutional Economics, have the effect of limiting the scope for government intervention. Together with the emergence of the Public Choice School, founded by James Buchanan, inefficiencies in the public sector are now largely explained in terms of rent-seeking arguments, or from a property rights/transaction cost economics perspective. Research interest in the market failures in the Sixties has been replaced by the interest in government failures. More importantly, in understanding the role of government and institutional change, cognitive learning and knowledge problems have been received greater attention than the past (e.g. Denzau and North 1994; North 1990). In particular, Chang (1994: 34-37) borrows Herbert Simon's bounded rationality concept to portray the government as machinery for coping with the limits of human comprehension and computation in the face of complexity and uncertainty. Despite these recent

[79] Coase's original article, namely, 'The Nature of the Firm' published in 1937, was not well received at that time. Coase's arguments have gained recognition only after he published his other significant piece of work, 'The Problem of Social Cost' in 1960.

contributions, in mainstream public economics, analysis of human action and learning in the public sector is virtually absent.[80] Ignoring uncertainty and knowledge, we cannot fully understand the underlying reasons for policy changes. Neglecting learning, trial and error and experimentation, one can easily blame incompetence of the government.[81]

In this chapter, I attempt to model the governmental process in the Austrian perspective. In particular, I shall apply the Schutzian theory of human agency to understand the decision making process in the public sector. The major components of the model consist of human action, opportunity discovery, learning, experimentation, revision of plans and error elimination. These elements are significant in understanding policy change. In what follows, the government[82] is viewed in the perspective of coordination economics (Section 7.2). The nature of a government organization and its capabilities is further explained in the Penrosian perspective (Section 7.3). The concept of human action in the public sector is introduced in Section 7.4, followed by propositions of human action in the public sector (Section 7.5). A Schutzian model of the decision making process of the public agent is presented in Section 7.6. Major implications of our arguments on policy change is presented in Section 7.7. It will be concluded that political agents, like their agents in the private sector, also make errors, learn, and revise plans and consequently, lead to policy change. This chapter suggests a new direction in research agenda in public economics (Section 7.8).

---

[80] In recent years, scholars in the New Public Management discipline has paid attention to learning problems in the government organization. In particular, Reschenthaler and Thompson (1998) apply a learning organization approach to understanding many of the problems of government in devising and implementing public policy. The arguments in my chapter, which apply Austrian economics and the theory of human agency in social science, can be complementary to the views from the Management discipline.

[81] This does not mean that we deny the existence of government failures and inefficiency.

[82] In this chapter, the term 'government' refers to any government organization, including ruling parties, government departments, bureaus or government-funded organization. It comes into being through the actions of individuals. The term 'government action' refers to action made by political agents in government organizations. Therefore, the phrase 'governments act' is merely a metaphor and must not be taken to mean that the collective institution itself has any reality apart from that acts of various individuals. In line with Max Weber (1947/1964), we take the point that only individual can act. See Von Mises (1949/1966: 43) and Rothbard (1962/1993: 2).

7.2 The government as a national coordinator

In the Austrian perspective, the government can be viewed as an institution for coordinating economic affairs. The capability of the market in coordinating economic activities is well documented in economics literatures. Yet, even the well-known libertarian scholars such as Hayek, Friedman and Buchanan do agree that there is a role for the government in economic affairs.[83] The reason is obvious. Successful coordination by the market is not always guaranteed. The failure of firms to coordinate economic activities (microeconomic phenomena) leads to economic recession, resulting in an increase in unemployment and a fall in national income (macroeconomic phenomena).[84] The view that the market fails because none is in charge is certainly not new. Scholars have already noted that decisions concerning resource allocations are made by thousands of different firms. With decision-making mutually interdependent on each other, it is difficult for a firm to plan. Without planning, resources cannot be efficiently allocated. Stiglitz and his colleagues (1989: 34) dispute that this argument does not justify the government control because intervention requires enormous amounts of information. In his view, the government is similar to the private sector which has only imperfect information. However, insufficient information does not preclude the need for a coordinator to help to work things out. On the contrary, it is essentially this reason that gives rise to government intervention. Interestingly, elsewhere Stiglitz (1996: 160) points out that in developing economies, the widespread absence of markets means that prices cannot perform their coordinating role. Thus, the government may have to assume a more

[83] Hayek and Friedman only accept the minimum role of the government as a nightwatcher.

[84] The analysis of the coordination of economic activities on aggregate levels has been examined by a group of Wicksellian followers. Leijonhufvud (1981) and Leijonhufvud and Clower (1981: 103-129) apply the information and coordination approach to interpret the massive unemployment in the Great Depression. For Leijonhufvud and Clower (1981: 119), the failure of the markets in general is due to the fact that the market is unable to transmit messages about desired transactions from one side to the other side. They refer to this phenomenon as 'effective demand failures'. In Leijonhufvud's view, Keynes' important contribution was to point out that there is a possibility that unemployment and real output would not be restored even after prices and money wages fall to their equilibrium levels. This situation, notably involuntary unemployment, arises if, during the adjustment to declining aggregate demand, households and firms both run out of backup sources of money. If both sets of transactors must depend on the receipts from their current sales for their money, unemployment will persist even after prices and wages have fallen. This was virtually the case of the Great Depression in 1929-1933. In Leijonhufvud and Clower's view, explicit government policy is needed to coordinate the plans of various groups of people. Changes in government expenditures and taxes are needed to bring the economy back into the 'safety corridor'. Thus, the government assumes a coordinating role in economic affairs.

active role in performing this function. Similarly, the World Bank (1997: 6) argues that when markets are underdeveloped, the state can sometimes reduce coordination problems and gaps in information. This implies that the more rapid the economic change, the greater the need for coordination – a view consistent with Silver's (1984) theory of the firm. This explains why heavy government intervention is observed in emerging economies where rapid economic changes occur in early stages of industrialization.[85] Like earlier studies (for example, Rosenstein-Rodan 1943), Stiglitz fails to further pursue the issue of the coordinative role of government action. The view of this chapter is that, complementary to the price mechanism, the government can at times perform the function of a coordinator when both markets and firms are impeded to do so.[86]

7.3 Government capabilities: resource-based and strategic planning

Capabilities of a government to coordinate economic activities depend on the resources that public managers can deploy. In the view of the resource-based school (Penrose 1959/1995; Richardson 1972; see also Yu and Robertson 2000), a government organization possesses a bundle of tangible and intangible collectively owned resources. These assets vary from department to department.[87] Apart from tangible items such as plant and equipment or the ownership of raw materials, they also extend to financial assets, knowledge, and behavior patterns. When viewed as a whole, therefore, the performance of the government is not only governed by its physical resources, but also by the public agents' ability to use those resources. This, in turn, is a function of what public officials know, both individually and collectively, and of how they interact with each other. In Nelson and Winter's terms (1982), the resources of a government organization are deployed according to the routines – the set of heuristics that the government organization has built up over time as efficient ways of undertaking common activities. These routines may be either a strength or a weakness depending on the prevailing conditions. When political agents are able to carry out activities successfully if the need arises, then the

85 Therefore, the Mercantilist Age, the post-war Japan and the Asian NIEs such as Taiwan, South Korea and Singapore serve to illustrate the coordinating role of the government.

86 Garzarelli and Limam (2002) discuss the vertical organization of the public sector in terms of knowledge coordination in the attempt to shed light on the organizational economics of federalism.

87 As Penrose (1959/1995) points out, all firms are, in fact, unique.

government can be regarded as possessing competences or capabilities.[88] In terms of 'strategic intent' (Hamel and Prahalad 1989), the government possesses a vision of future outcomes in which its economy outperforms its competitors and becomes highly successful. In short, recent developments in organizational theories can apply to understand the working of the government.

7.3.1 Action and planning under uncertainty

A private firm needs planning and so does the government. Austrian economists, in the tradition of Von Mises (1949/1966) and Hayek (1935), argue the impossibility of central planning.[89] In their views, without market prices signal as a guidance, it is impossible to do economic calculation, and hence impossible to do planning. Accordingly, resources cannot be allocated efficiently by using non-market measures (Klein 1996: 11). Such view is later summarized by Salerno (1990: 52) who notes, 'without recourse to calculating and comparing the benefits and costs of production using the structure of monetary prices determined at each moment on the market, the human mind is only capable of surveying, evaluating, and directing production processes whose scope is drastically reduced to the compass of the primitive household economy'. Hence, the larger the size of the government, the less the economy is relied on the market mechanism. It follows that socialism, which applies central planning, is doomed to fail. However, the impossibility of central planning does not imply that the government, as an organization, does not need to plan. Given that a government is required in every economy, and given that it is an administrative organization, then planning must be needed in formulating any public project, though the objectives of the public project are not profits or monetary gains, but for some social goals. In this sense, measuring the government performance is no longer in terms of profit, but other achievement indexes such as the degree of equality in the society. In short, central planning is impossible, but planning is indispensable for any rational organization, including a government organization.

In terms of national growth and international competitiveness, political agents need to formulate development strategies for their nation with the aim of building up nation's competitive advantage. A sound government policy, just like a corporate business policy, requires planning, involving

[88] The term 'capabilities' was originally used by Richardson (1972).

[89] This is a famous socialist debate between Hayek, Von Mises and Lange in the 1920s. For a review of central planning controversies, see Lavoie (1985).

the selection of strategies.[90] According to Porter (1990: 45), the source of competitive advantage arises out of entrepreneur's perception or discovery of better ways to compete in an industry. Thus, the government, as a social coordinator can enhance a nation's competitive advantage by conceiving new ways of conducting activities, employing new procedures, new technologies or different inputs (Porter 1990: 41). In creating a nation's competitive advantage, references can be made to the economy's resource bases which cover not only on physical resources, but also the government's ability to use these resources. If the public manager wants to formulate a development strategy, what will be the likely procedure to arrive a decision? We use the Austrian theory of human agency to explain the behavior of public managers and the governmental process.

7.4 The governmental process: an Austrian perspective

Austrian economics has tremendous insight into the market process.[91] They stress on knowledge and coordination problems, and develop powerful tools in understanding the economic world. Unfortunately, constrained by their ideologies, Austrian economists refuse to apply their insights in understanding the government. It is well known that Austrian economics is in defense of private property rights and attacks any form of government intervention. They refuse to investigate into the nature of the government, public agent's behavior and political process.[92] Instead, they devote their research efforts exclusively to negative aspects of government intervention, namely rent-seeking, corruption and inefficiency (to name a few). However, ideologies aside, there is no reason why we cannot use the Austrian approach and insight to explain the government behavior, decision making in the public sector, and the related government phenomena. In this chapter, instead of trying to examine the political institution as a unit of organization, we take Buchanan's (1979: 157) path breaking approach in

---

[90] For an exposition of planning as learning, see De Geus (1988).

[91] Rosen (1997) argues that the theory of entrepreneur is one of the biggest strengths of the Austrian school. Modeling political agents – whether they are voters, bureaucrats, or politicians – as entrepreneurs is a significant area in which Austrian applications to political economy can establish empirical relevance (see also Boettke 2002: 114).

[92] It must be noted that Fredrich Von Weiser (1914/1967) contributes to the theory of public economy.

public economics[93] which 'examine the interactions among individuals as they carry out assigned roles within these institutions'. Austrian theories can contribute to governmental economics in the sense that the school has a long tradition in trying to understand purposive human action. The nature of political agents' actions is to be examined below.

7.4.1 Political agents: self interest or public interest?

The most controversial and crucial element in analyzing the role of the government is the assumption of human agency in the public sector. Mid-century scholars assume the government agency with public interest. Following Adam Smith, most Chicago school economists view all individuals in the society as selfish. James Buchanan, the founder of the Public Choice School, assumes that political agents, like private agents, are also self interest and his new position starts a turning point in studying government. Following Knight (1921) and Von Mises (1949/1966), we argue that human agents, be they in private or public sector, act. Action is a 'person's conscious adjustment to the state of the universe that determines his/her life' (Von Mises 1949/1966: 11). Moreover, an acting individual is always eager to substitute a more satisfactory state of affairs for a less satisfactory one. The incentive that makes a person to act is always some uneasiness. What makes a person feel uneasy and less uneasy is established by that person from the standard of his/her own will and judgement, from his/her personal and subjective valuation and nobody is in a position to decree what should make a fellow person happier (Von Mises 1949/1966: 14). This argument does not refer in any way to the notion of self interest or public interest. There are people whose only aim is to improve the condition of their own ego. There are other people with whom awareness of the troubles of their fellow men causes as much uneasiness as or even more uneasiness than their own wants. Some people are more concerned with material wants but other people care more with social images, such as being a patriotic or religious person. It follows that an action is entirely rational if it aims, at the expenses of material and tangible advantages, at the attainment of ideal or cultural satisfactions. Given that the governmental goal and personal goal of a political agent need not be the same, a political agent in most case acts partly for some material wants such as better income, promotions etc and partly for the government organization. In

[93] James Buchanan is regarded as the founder of Public Choice School. His methodology and his works are consistent with the Austrian approach. However, most works in the Public Choice School nowadays use the neoclassical methodology. Hence, it can be claimed that the Public Choice School is divided into two streams: neoclassical and neo-Austrian.

short, a public official has many goals. He/She always aims at improving his/her own state of satisfaction, replacing a less satisfactory state of affairs with a more satisfactory one.[94]

7.4.2 Human actions are socially embedded

In neoclassical economics, the world consists of the unbounded antagonistic moves of independent actors (Abolafia and Biggart 1992). Actors are isolated units and that social relations are frictionless. In Abolafia and Biggart's terms (1992: 316-317), the neoclassical modeling of an economy is 'transhistoric and acultural'. Unlike the neoclassical formulation, the approach presented here maintains that human action has underlying norms and is sustained by institutional arrangements (Abolafia and Biggart 1992: 315). Individuals, either in the private or public sector, have intersubjective orientations: they recognize each other as contestants and observe each other closely. As Granovetter (1985: 487) notes, 'actors do not behave or decide as atoms outside a social context ... Their attempts at purposive action are instead embedded in concrete, ongoing systems of social relations'. Applying the socio-economic insight, the government process is thus understood as actions structured by a specific political, economic and cultural context.[95]

7.5 Propositions regarding the public agent's action

Utilizing the theory of human action developed by Weber (1947/1964: 87-118) and Von Mises (1949/1966: 1-71), and elaborated by Rothbard (1962/1993: 1-6), propositions regarding actions made by political agents are presented as follows:

1. All political agents have goals. All actions made by political agents are purposive. However, their goals need not be the same with the government organization, though public agents are supposed to work for governmental goals.
2. Public sector agents engage in conscious actions toward chosen goals. To reach the goals, means must be employed. The agents have consciously

[94] In this sense, actions are always self-interest. Even if an action aims at improving other person's condition can be regarded as self interest.

[95] For example, government intervention in the South Korean economy can be understood as an expression of Korean patrimonialism (Biggart and Orru, 1997; Biggart and Guillen, 1999). Under patrimonialism, the economy is regarded as a 'household' under the unilateral domination of a patrimonial figurehead or leader. All members of the household must submit to the orders of the patriarch, to whom they owe obedience and personal loyalty.

chosen certain means to reach their goals. Since efforts have been made to reach the goals, the goals must have value to the agents.
3. Public agents believe that they employ the technologically correct method of reaching the goals. The human action approach does not assume that public agents' choices of values or goals are wise, proper, or correct. All it argues is that they believe, given their knowledge, they have chosen the best method to achieve the targets. Hence, a person's experience and knowledge are important factors in action formations.
4. All actions conducted by political agents take place through time. In other words, all their actions take place in the present and are directed toward the future attainment of an end. The emphasis of the role of time implies that government policies make a difference. It also implies that the agents do not possess perfect knowledge of the future. If they had such knowledge, no action would have been taken, since it would not make a difference. In sum, all public actors, like those in the private sector, live in a world of an uncertain future and choose to employ means according to a technological plan in the present they expect to arrive at the goals at some future time.

7.6 Modeling the decision-making process in the public sector

In a largely neglected work,[96] Downs (1967: 175-176) presents a model of the decision making process inside a bureau in the following non-programming steps: (1) perception, (2) assimilation, (3) performance assessment, (4) formulation, analysis and evaluation of alternatives, (5) strategy formulation, (6) action selection, (7) re-assessment of the action taken from data feedback. In Downs' model, information is passively received by the agent, though such information may change the outlook of the agent's world. We feel that human agents are not only simply concerned with solving a pre-determined pattern of economic problems, but rather creating a state of affairs which is geared toward their advantage. As Shackle (1969) notes, the future is not only discovered, but must be created. Public agents create the future so as to make it controllable (Harper 1996: 57). Applying the Schutzian theory of human agency, the decision making

[96] Anthony Downs can be regarded as one of the forerunners of governmental economics. His seminal work, *An Economic Theory of Democracy* (1957) has laid the foundation for the economic of voting. However, his other brilliant work, *Inside Bureaucracy* (1967) has largely been neglected. In an authoritative survey in public choice, Mueller (1989) does not cite this work at all.

process exerted by public agents in a government organization involves four main mental stages, namely (see Chapter 2):
1. projecting an opportunity idea;
2. selective attention;
3. elaboration of an opportunity;
4. implementing a project.

As in the market process, the governmental process is basically a mental projection, exercised by the imaginations of public officials. At the infant stage of mental projection, public agents envisage a new project or a new method of implementing a policy. At this stage, they do not necessarily intend to carry it out. They simply mentally apply new ideas to their anticipated future before deciding whether or not to try it. The imagined content is shaped by their past experiences and knowledge (Schutz 1970: 125-159; Weigert 1981: 139).

Facing complexity in the everyday life and the possibility of the projection of many imagined worlds, public agents will allocate their attention between current operations and prospective new projects, depending on the relative attractiveness of the two projects (Gifford 1992: 176-178). Thus, public officials tend to expose themselves to ideas that are in accordance with their interests, needs, or existing attitudes. They consciously or unconsciously avoid messages that are in conflict with their predispositions.

Individuals can imagine but not everyone can put ideas into reality. Public agents would try to formulate plans which they can realize. Like private enterprises, public agents encounter two practicability problems in transforming their imaginations into reality (Schutz and Luckmann 1989): first, the estimation of the objective conditions for reaching their goals, and second, the estimation of their own capacities to carry out the act. For a perceived opportunity to be feasible, public managers must believe that they can transform what they project into reality. This is based on a general assumption that today is essentially the same as yesterday and there will be a tomorrow like today (Schutz and Luckmann 1989: 25-26).

When a public official has several projects in hand before taking an action, how is the decision made? Mainstream neoclassical scholars would recommend the use of the cost and benefit analysis to select a public program. Not denying the usefulness of the technique, the choice of a public program is ultimately determined by the preferences of government agents which are in turn determined by their experience and knowledge. Like the decision making process in the private sector, the choice between conflicting projects for public agents is essentially an act of interpretation. According to Schutz and Luckmann (1989: 47), choosing is an interpretative decision made under the pressure of action and time in an actual present situation. Furthermore, the decision process itself is future oriented. Assume two projects, that is, two alternative futures, A and B. First, assume that A is projected by the public agent in the future perfect tense. Next, B is also projected in the same manner. Both are retained, reproduced and compared. If project A is perceived to be clearly superior to the other, then the decision can be made. Furthermore, any end is only a means towards another end and any project is projected within a system of higher order. Therefore choices between projects refer to a previously chosen system of connected projects of a higher order (Schutz 1970: 146-159).[97]

7.7 The government as a learning agent: error elimination, revision of plans and policy change

When a public project fails, neoclassical public choice scholars often interpret this as a result of rent-seeking activities. While this may be true in some cases, their analysis generally overlooks one important element, namely structural uncertainty. Given such uncertainty, public agents initiating a new public project would encounter similar difficulties to private entrepreneurs in their decision making. Therefore, planning and implementing a new public program also involves learning, trial and error, experimentation and revisions of plans. As argued, behavior of the political entrepreneur is 'alertness to unnoticed opportunities to achieve policy outcomes.' In this perspective, Lachmann's contribution (1956) to the market process can be well applied to the public sector. Government action, like private agents, exists in the form of plans which ultimately link with the stock of knowledge possessed by public policy makers (Lachmann 1970: 36). The subjective interpretation of problematic situation by government officials yields provisional judgements to be confirmed by subsequent experience, imperfect knowledge capable of being perfected. The formation of plans is therefore nothing but a phase in the continuous process of exchange and transmission of knowledge which effectively integrates an economy. Each plan does not stand by itself, but is the cumulative result of a series of expectations which have been revised

97 In simple terms, plans are hierarchical (Lachmann 1970; Langlois 1986). For a more complicated decision regarding the plan hierarchy, see Schutz and Luckmann (1989: 39-42).

in the light of later experience, and these past revisions are the source of present knowledge. On the other hand, the current plans to be revised later as experience accrues are not only the basis of the action plans but also a source of improved future knowledge. A new problem situation requires the public planner to invent new trial solutions which are then subjected to further testing in the real world. The process continues indefinitely, so that a series of new problems and new plans gradually bring about progress in the public officials' knowledge. The formation of plans is thus a continuous process, an element of the larger process of the transmission of knowledge (Lachmann 1956).

Further insights on the decision making process in the public sector can be gained by applying Harper's (1996) growth of knowledge theory. Like private business people, public policy makers are constantly engaged in solving problems which tend to involve much novelty and which are ill-specified (Harper 1994: 56). Whenever actual events diverge from their predictions, government decision makers learn that something is wrong with their stock of knowledge. They know that they cannot hold on to their existing conjectural framework (Harper 1994: 63). Simply put, the failure of a plan must be due to inadequate knowledge of the circumstances in which the action has to be taken. Previously unsuccessful policies prompt the need for a revision of government plans. A new array of plans is formed, each with a tentative solution to the original problem. The number or variety of solutions proposed is limited by the public manager's creativity and imagination (Harper 1994: 71). The new plan too is problematic. Each trial solution is controlled by a process of attempted error-elimination. Error elimination is done through the testing of ideas in practice, which involves the comparison and assessment of rival conjectures in terms of how well they can solve the problems (Harper 1994: 72). In short, given uncertainty and knowledge problems, public agents, like private agents, will revise plans. By trial and error, those policy options accepted by majority voters will be adopted, while rejected by voters will be discarded. In this way, a policy change can be viewed as a result of a mutual adjustment process of continuous interpretations of external information and plan revisions among all political agents and voters in the economy.

7.8 Conclusion

Owing to the fact that the analysis of human action in the public sector is lacking in neoclassical mainstream, new institutional and neoclassical public choice paradigms, this chapter attempts to fill such gap. This chapter applies the Austrian theory of human agency to analyze political agents' actions and the decision making process in the public sector. Our perspective does not attempt to replace any of the above paradigms but complement them by inserting Austrian elements, such as discovery, learning and plan revisions in interpreting the government behavior and hence policy change. Unlike the neoclassical economics which assumes static uncertainty,[98] our Austrian perspective deals with structural uncertainty.[99] Thus, given genuine uncertainty, political agents perceive external events and formulate plans according to their experience and knowledge. With new information and experience, they subsequently revise their plans in order to eliminate errors. This governmental process which involves subjectivist learning is 'more than mathematical computation, rather it consists of the setting up of the problem situation itself or the movement from one problem situation to another' (O'Driscoll and Rizzo 1985: 37). It takes place when the agent's framework of interpreting external messages of stimuli has changed over time. Once the concept of structural uncertainty and knowledge problems are introduced in economic analysis, the whole government policy framework becomes a dynamic process. More importantly, our perspective suggests that the impact of a government policy on the economy in the future is not deterministic. In other words, we can never know definitely what the consequence of a government policy will be.[100] Many government policies yield a surprise to the economy and result in institutional change. It is a surprise because human agency is creative. Through trial and error, experimentation and learning, a new policy and hence, a new regime emerges and replaces the old one. It can be concluded that both market and government sectors cruise into the journal of an unknown future.[101]

---

[98] According to Arrow (1974: 33), uncertainty in conventional neoclassical sense refers to the situation 'that we do not have a complete description of the world which we fully believe to be true. Instead, we consider the world to be in one or another of a range of states. Each state of the world is a description which is complete for all relevant purposes'. This sort of uncertainty consists in not knowing which state is the true one.

[99] Structural uncertainty refers not only to the situation that people do not know the chances of various outcomes, but that they do not know what outcomes are possible. They may well be far from sure even of the structures of the problem that they face (Loasby 1976: 9).

[100] Menger (1883 [1985]) argues that institutions are 'the unintended result of innumerable efforts of economic subjects pursuing individual interests'. Hayek (1979: 150) elaborates that 'many of the greatest things man has achieved are the result not of consciously directed thought, and still less the product of a deliberately coordinated effort of many individuals, but of a process in which the individual plays a part which he can never fully understand'.

[101] The rise and fall of the socialist system in the human history is one example. See Yu (2001).

References

Abolafia, M. and N. Biggart (1992) Competitive Systems: a Sociological View. In P. Ekins and M. Max-Neef (eds.) *Real-Life Economics: Understanding Wealth Creation*. London, UK: Routledge, pp. 315-323.

Arrow, K. (1974) *The Limits of Organisation*. New York, USA: Norton.

Biggart, N.W. and M. Orru (1997) Societal Strategic Advantage: Automotive and Electronics Industries in East Asia. In: A. Bugru and B. Usdiken (eds.) *State, Market and Organizational Forms*. Berlin, Germany: de Gruyer, pp. 201-239.

Biggart, N.W. and M.F. Guillen (1999) Developing Difference: Social Organization and the Rise of the Auto Industries of South Korea, Taiwan, Spain and Argentina. *American Sociological Review*, vol. 64: 722-747.

Boettke, P.J. (2002) Austrian Economics and Public Choice. *The Review of Austrian Economics*, vol. 15 (2/3): 111-119.

Buchanan, J. (1979) An Economic Approach to 'Scientific Politics'. In: *What Should Economists Do*. Indianapolis, USA: Liberty Press, 143-159.

Chang, H-J. (1994) *The Political Economy of Industrial Policy*. New York, USA: St. Martin Press.

Cheung, S.N.S. (1983) The Contractual Nature of the Firm. *The Journal of Law and Economics*, vol. 26: 386-405.

Cheung, S.N.S. (1989) *Essays on the Three Systems*. Hong Kong, China PR: Hong Kong Economic Times.

Coase, R. (1937) The Nature of the Firm. *Economica*, vol. 4, 386-405.

Coase, R. (1960) The Problem of Social Cost. *Journal of Law and Economics*, vol. 3, 1-44.

De Geus, A.P. (1988) Planning as Learning. *Harvard Business Review*, vol. 66 (2), 70-74.

Denzau, A.T. and D.C. North (1994) Shared Mental Models: Ideologies and Institutions. *Kyklos*, vol. 47 (1), 3-31.

Downs, A. (1957) *An Economic Theory of Democracy*. New York, USA: Harper and Row.

Downs, A. (1967) *Inside Bureaucracy*. Boston, USA: Little Brown.

Garzarelli, G. and Y.R. Limam (2002) Coordination, Knowledge, and Supranational Federalism: An Organizational Perspective. Paper presented at the XIV Siep conference, University of Pavia, 4-5 October 2002.

Gifford, S. (1992) Allocation of Entrepreneurial Attention. *Journal of Economic Behaviour and Organisation*, vol. 19, 265-83.

Granovetter, M. (1985) Economic Action and Social Structure: The Problem of Embeddedness. *The American Journal of Sociology*, vol. 91, 481-510.

Hamel, G. and C.K. Prahalad (1989) Strategic Intent. *Harvard Business Review*, vol. 67 (3), 63-76.

Harper, D.A. (1994) A New Approach to Modelling Endogenous Learning Processes In Economic Theory. In: P. Boettke, I. Kirzner and M. Rizzo (eds.) *Advances in Austrian Economics I*. Greenwich, USA: JAI Press.

Harper, D.A. (1996) *Entrepreneurship and the Market Process: An Enquiry into the Growth of Knowledge*. London, UK: Routledge.

Hayek, F.A. (1935) *Collectivist Economic Planning*. London, UK: Routledge.

Hayek, F.A. (1979) *The Counter-Revolution of Science*. Indianapolis, USA: Liberty Press.

Klein, P. (1996) Economic Calculation and the Limits of Organisation. *The Review of Austrian Economics*, vol. 9 (2), 3-28.

Knight, F. (1921) *Risk, Uncertainty and Profit*. Boston, USA: Houghton Fifflin.

Lachmann, L.M. (1970) *The Legacy of Max Weber*. London, UK: Heinemann.

Langlois, R.N. (1986) Coherence and Flexibility: Social Institutions in a World of Radical Uncertainty. In: I.M. Kirzner (ed.) *Subjectivism, Intelligibility and Economic Understanding*, New York, USA: New York University Press.

Lavoie, D. (1985) *Rivalry and Central Planning, the Social Calculation Debate Reconsidered*, Cambridge, UK: Cambridge University Press.

Leijonhufvud, A. (1981) *Information and Coordination*. Oxford, UK: Oxford University Press.

Leijonhufvud, A. and R. Clower (1973/1981) Effective Demand Failures. *Swedish Journal of Economics*, vol. 75, 27-48. Reprinted in: A. Leijonhufvud (1981), *Information and Coordination*. Oxford, UK: Oxford University Press.

Loasby, B.J. (1976) *Choice, Complexity and Ignorance*, Cambridge: Cambridge University Press.

Menger, C. (1883[1985]) *Investigations into the Method of the Social Sciences with Special Reference to Economics*. New York, USA: New York University Press.

Von Mises, L. (1949/1966) *Human Action: A Treatise on Economics*. 3rd edition. Chicago, USA: Contemporary Books.

Mueller, D. (1989) *Public Choice II*. Cambridge, UK: Cambridge University Press.

Nelson, R.R. and S.G. Winter (1982) *An Evolutionary Theory of Economic Change*. Cambridge, USA: Harvard University Press.

North, D. (1990) *Institutions, Institutional Change and Economic Performance*. Cambridge, UK: Cambridge University Press.

O'Driscoll Jr., G. and M. Rizzo (1985) *The Economics of Time and Ignorance*. Oxford, UK: Blackwell.

Penrose, E. (1959/1995) *The Theory of the Growth of the Firm*. Oxford, UK: Basil Blackwell.

Porter, M.E. (1990) *The Competitive Advantage of Nations*. New York, USA: The Free Press.

Reschenthaler, G.B. and F. Thompson (1998) Public Management and the Learning Organization. *International Public Management Journal*, vol. 1 (1), 59-106.

Richardson, G. (1972) The Organisation of Industry. *Economic Journal*, vol. 82, 883-896.
Rosen, S. (1997) Austrian and Neoclassical Economics: Any Gains from Trade? *Journal of Economic Perspective*, vol. 4, 139-152.
Rosenstein-Rodan, P.N. (1943) Problems of Industrialisation in Eastern and South Eastern Europe. *Economic Journal*, vol. 53, 202-211.
Rothbard, M.N. (1962/1993) *Man, Economy and State.* Auburn, USA: Ludwig Von Mises Institute.
Salerno, J.T. (1990) *Postscript to Reprint of Mises 1920.* Auburn, USA: Ludwig Von Mises Institute.
Schutz, A. (1970) *On Phenomenology and Social Relations.* Chicago, USA: The University of Chicago Press.
Schutz, A. and T. Luckmann (1989) *The Structures of the Life World.* Evanston, USA: Northwestern University Press, Volume II.
Shackle, G.L.S. (1969) *Decision, Order, and Time in Human Affairs.* Cambridge, UK: Cambridge University Press.
Silver, M. (1984) *Enterprise and the Scope of the Firm.* London, UK: Martin Robertson.
Stiglitz, J.E. (1996) Some Lessons from the East Asian Miracle. *The World Bank Research Observer*, vol. 11 (2), 151-177.
Stiglitz, J.E. (1989) *The Economic Role of the State.* Oxford, UK: Blackwell.
Von Wieser, F. (1914/1967) *Social Economics.* New York, USA: A.M. Kelly.
Weber, M. (1947/1964) *The Theory of Social and Economic Organisation.* New York, USA: The Free Press.
Weigert, A.J. (1981) *Sociology of Everyday Life.* New York, USA: Longman.
World Bank (1997) *The State in a Changing World. World Development Report.* Oxford, UK: Oxford University Press.
Yu, T.F-L. and P.L. Robertson (2000) Technological Capabilities and the Strategies of Small Manufacturing Firms: The Case of Hong Kong. In: N.J. Foss and P.L. Robertson (eds.) *Resource, Strategy and Technology.* London, UK: Routledge, pp. 227-251.
Yu, T.F-L. (2001) An Entrepreneurial Perspective of Institutional Change. *Constitutional Political Economy*, vol. 12 (3), 217-236.

Chapter 8.
A new perspective on transition

8.1 Introduction

The dramatic abandonment of central planning as principal mode of organizing economic activities in Russia, Central and Eastern European Bloc and the Mainland China has triggered scholars' interest in economics of transition.[102] Unfortunately, more than ten years after the fall of the Berlin Wall, we are still relatively ignorant on the economics of transition (Roland 2001). Significant disagreements regarding the issues of transition still remain. Despite growing literatures on transition in recent years, the concept of transition is still very much in poverty.[103] It continues to be popular to say that there is no theory to guide the practical process of transition, only theories of capitalism and socialism (Havrylyshyn 2001: 54). Kornai (2000) even goes further to claim that transition by definition does not need a paradigm or theory – only the beginning and end-point systems do.

The mainstream neoclassical economists regard transition economies suffering from severe economic distortion.[104] Therefore, their main objective is to advise these economies 'to get the prices right'. Ignoring genuine uncertainty, learning and the process of change, they equate equilibrium with economic stability.[105] In the neoclassical view, transition occurs between two equilibrium states and is unstable. Transition

[102] According to International Monetary Fund (IMF 2001: 185), transition economies including Commonwealth of Independent States (CIS), Central and Eastern Europe, China and Mongolia account for 17.5% of the world output and 27.8% of the world population.

[103] The term 'transition economies' seems not yet clearly defined in the literature. Most conventional view implicitly defines a transition economy as an economy moving towards a market style of economy (IMF 2001: 127). IMF (2001: 129) constructs an aggregate transition indicator to show the extent of these economies toward a market economy. In the Austrian perspective, Colombatto (2002: 61) defines 'transition as the period of time it takes for new institutions and organizations to be introduced and upheld, for agents to learn how to operate according to a reformed system of property rights and adjust to hitherto virtually unknown rules of the game'.

[104] In particular, Kierzkowski (1997: 5) argues that transition is a 'move from a position well inside the 'production possibility frontier' to a more efficient position closer to the frontier'. Similar neoclassical approach is applied by Havrylyshyn (2001: 82-83).

[105] For an entrepreneurial critique of mainstream neoclassical policies on development, see Yu (1998: 353-372).

economies eventually need to move toward a stable equilibrium. For instance, Roland and Verdier (2000) draw attention to a social coordination problem associated with law enforcement in transition economies. Their model concludes that multiple equilibra can occur. Hence, for Roland and Verdier, a policy prescription for transition economies is to eliminate bad equilibrium. In general, the neoclassical policy package is designed to transform transition economies from centrally-planned economies operating under the socialist system into market-type economies operating under the capitalist system in a democratic political framework. Neglecting institutional issue, neoclassical authors believe that 'once central planning was swept away, it was taken for granted that the opening of markets would bring with it – rather quickly and painlessly – the needed institutional structures to market the new market system work properly' (Hare 2001: 77). The mainstream neoclassical view has been taken up by influential international policy makers represented by the Washington Consensus[106] and was dominant at the beginning of the transition period in Central and Eastern Europe. Focusing on allocative efficiency, the Washington Consensus view has strong faith in social engineering (Roland 2001: 32). A striking feature of the economic strategies and policies given to transition economies by these western economic advisors is the extent to which they are grounded in neoclassical economic theory and divorced from the historical legacies, and the related political and social realities (Weisskopf 1997: 309). Built upon the neoclassical price theories and stabilization policy, the Washington Consensus view fails to come to grips with the historical legacy of these societies, and therefore unable to explain many phenomena occurred in transition economies. Not surprisingly, these policy makers have been shocked by the huge fall in output after price liberalization and the continuous economic decline in Russia and other countries of the former Soviet Union.

8.2 Contributions from new institutional economics[107]

In recent years, new institutional economics, evidenced by the success of China's reform, has gained much ground in the transition debate. Emphasizing on the process of change and transaction costs, the new institutional theory focuses on one important element of economic change, namely the structure of property rights, which sets the constraints

[106] The Washington Consensus view is in general associated with the views of the IMF and World Bank. It is initially coined by John Williamson in 1990 (Roland 2001: 31).

[107] Roland (2001) terms new institutional economics as the evolutionary institutional view.

or rules for people to compete and exchange.[108] In the new institutional perspective, it can be argued that transition occurs when a set of property rights of an economy transforms into another set, or more specifically, from one type of incentives to another. Since the change in the structure of property rights takes time, the transition period is therefore a long and evolutionary process. Though the new institutional perspective is undoubtedly much closer to reality than the neoclassical mathematical modeling in explaining transition phenomena, it does not escape some neoclassical pitfalls articulated in the concept of efficiency and equilibrium. Using the concept of transaction costs, new institutional scholars are able to argue that the communist regime is inefficient and therefore should be abandoned. They strongly endorse market mechanism, which builds upon the private property rights, as a mean of organizing economic activities. So for new institutional scholars, transition implies a change from the communist regime (communal property rights) to the market system (private property rights). They accordingly prescribe a policy package of liberalization of economies and privatization of state-owned enterprises. Though the new institutional view has provided us with a better understanding of transition, human agency has never been its centre of analysis. More specifically, they generally ignore entrepreneurship, human creativity and learning, though some of recent transaction costs literatures have begun to pay more attention on mental construct.[109] More importantly, new institutional economists are never interested in asking why communism was taken place at the beginning. As Popovic (2001: 95) correctly asks in a transition forum, 'what is the driving force of an institutional reform'? It should be stressed that it is imaginative human agency that breaks down an old system and creates a new one. Utilizing the transaction costs concept, new institutional economists may be able to explain in general the direction of change, but not the origin of change. Moreover, if we take the notion of human creativity seriously, then all economic systems are unique. No regime in the real world is identical because no two human races interpret things in the same way. In this sense, all transition economies move into an unknown future (see below). Given human creativeness, each transition economy is heading towards something that its people do not know in advance and the market system may not be the final destination for these transition economies.

---

[108] The property rights approach to transition becomes very popular in recent years. See *Le Journal des Economistes et des Etudes Humaines*, vol. 11(1), March 2001.

[109] For example, see Denzau and North (1994); Mantzavinos *et al.* (2001).

In this chapter, we shall present an Austrian perspective of transition. Hitherto, little research has been conducted in the subjectivist paradigm. The only recent work that I am aware of is by Colombatto (2002: 61-74) who attempts to explain transition in Austrian economics. Adopting the Hayekian view, he analyses transition in terms of three criteria: acquisition of knowledge, individual responsibility and free entry into the market place. In Colombatto's view, transition economies should be subordinate to the analysis of the changes in the opportunity sets and to the willingness of the actors to take advantages of such new opportunities. Accordingly, an external shock is perceived as the moment when new sets of opportunities are made available to the individual. Colombatto has correctly analyzed transition in terms of knowledge problems – the element that Austrian economists always emphasize. However, focusing on opportunities and constraints, Colombatto's arguments look very similar to the new institutional view. Colombatto, unfortunately, has not explained transition in Austrian subjectivism in the full extent. In this chapter, transition is defined as a process of transforming the society's stock of knowledge. The novelty of this chapter is that transition is explained in terms of subjectivist elements such as perception, learning, errors, expectation, experimentation and creativity.

The Austrian approach to transition developed in this chapter builds upon theory of human action and starts with a mental construct. Thus human institutions, or society's stocks of knowledge, are viewed as the unintended consequence of coordinating effort of human action.[110] Transition means change in institutions which is the result of change in people's perception. Stability in institutions refers to the situation that people collectively articulate the same stock of social knowledge and make similar interpretation to the external world without any difficulty. This framework will shed light on two important issues: (1) the resistance of change during the transition period and (2) on the debate between two types of reforms, namely, 'gradualism' and 'shock therapy'. In what follows, a theoretical framework of transition in term of human perception, learning and classification is constructed. This framework is applied to explain the meaning and the nature of transition, and some economic phenomena observed in transition economies.

[110] Carl Menger first used the terms economizing man in his *Principles of Economics* (1871/1994). In the same vein, Hayek argues that human institutions are the unintended consequence of economizing human action. In Austrian tradition, since economizing means coordination (Yu 1999: 25-41), therefore, it is more correctly to claim that human institutions are the unintended consequence of coordinating effort of human action.

8.3 Classifying external events: the Hayekian perspective

In a classic cognitive work, Hayek (1952) argues that the process of perception of external events is a complicated undertaking, involving the capacity to identify, imitate and internalize patterns and transfer perception across domains of space and time. Before interpretation is taken place, agents have to identify certain events, some of which may have never been observed before. However, it is unlikely that phenomena are completely novel; rather they are likely to resemble something that has been previously experienced (Hayek 1952; see also Fleetwood 1995: 111). This sensory perception is described by Hayek (1952: 104) as 'an act of classification'. In other words, the human mind is able to classify sensory elements and recognize patterns as 'one of the same kind' even though it has never been experienced before. During the perception process, the mind is building up a record of past stimuli or, more accurately, of associations or connections between stimuli with which to compare new incoming stimuli. In Hayek's (1952: 142) words:

'what we perceive can never be unique properties of individual objects but always only properties which the objects have in common with other objects. Perception is thus always an interpretation, the placing of something into one or several classes of objects'.

If the event and subsequent stimulus have been repeated with some minimal regularly, a pattern will begin to register in the mind. Each time when the same event and subsequent stimuli is experienced, the same following is excited. This means that the impulse travels via the same route, forming the same linkage and establishing the same following. The result is that these events are classified as the same (Fleetwood 1995: 115). It is worth iterating that perception is founded upon the experience of a person. All that is perceived is immediately confronted with classes of already recorded data. Every perception of a new stimulus, or class of stimuli, will be influenced by previous implemented classifications. A new phenomenon will always be perceived in association with other events with which it has something in common (Hayek 1952: 142-143).

8.4 Rules and institutions: cost-saving device

Due to the limits of our reason, we follow rules. Rules are the device for coping with our ignorance. The whole rationale of rule-guided action is to be found in our inescapable ignorance of most of particular circumstances which determine the effects of our actions (Hayek 1967: 90). Rules facilitate the decision-making in complex situations. They limit our range of choice by reducing the list of circumstances which we need to take into account in particular circumstances, singling out certain classes of facts as alone determining the general kind of action which we should take (Hayek 1964: 11). In Hayek's words (1962: 56-57):

> 'Rules, tacitly understood and unconsciously followed, will often merely determine or limit the range of possibilities within which the choice is made consciously. By eliminating certain kinds of action altogether and providing certain routine ways of achieving the object, they merely restrict the alternatives on which a conscious choice is required.
>
> The moral rules, for example, which have become part of a man's nature will mean that certain conceivable choices will not appear at all among the possibilities between which he chooses ... [The] rules which guide an individual's action are better seen as determining what he will not do rather than what he will do.'

Hence, 'rules ... do not govern only our actions. They also govern our perception, and particularly our perceptions of other people's actions' (Hayek 1962: 45). Institutions or 'rules of doing things' can be regarded as *common schemes of behavior,* which simplify the complexity of the world and enable us to operate with a certain degree of predictability. They standardize the world and help to solve problems during social interactions. Different individuals act inside the world and within its limits, which ensure order and a certain regularity through simplification. Transition in the subjectivist perspective is thus a process of which new rules replace old rules, or new thinking displaces old thinking. In the next section, we shall explore in detail how the process of transition is initiated and completed.

8.5 New opportunities, mental process and economic transition

Human agents are not passive robots. They do not only adapt themselves to the external world but also adjust the environment to their needs through deliberate and conscious choices. Besides being diffusers and users of knowledge, agents are also a source of knowledge. In other words, they are builders and users of knowledge, creators of economic processes and above all, the engine of change (Hayek 1952; see also Rizzello 1999; 2000). In this sense, economic change is connected with the fact that human agents constantly create the reasons for their own existence, try to have influences as much as possible and thus to determine the future states of the world in a direction that favors their own development (Rizzello 2000: 127-150). Suppose an external event creates impulses to the perception process. New impulses will not be acted upon immediately in a stimulus-response manner or this would produce erratic behavior. Instead, they will be assessed by the mind to see how these new events fit into the total picture of the agent's mind. Selection of the appropriate response involves not only responding to one impulse with one action, but also drawing upon previous record of associations (Fleetwood 1995: 115). If some completely new pattern of events cannot be classified, then the mental process enters a transitional stage. Agents are unable to perceive and classify action that they may have never seen before, and thereby initiate an appropriate response action. It follows that a mechanism of sensory pattern transfer is in operation. In other words, a pattern learned in one format is transferred to another so that a pattern is recognized in a different format. Without the capacity to transfer a pattern across fields, agents would be incapable of perceiving any kind of novel behavior (Fleetwood 1995: 112).

However, the established linkages of the mental map often fail to give an adequate account of the current or immediate-future environment in which agents find themselves (i.e. a wrong prediction). In other words, the stock of existing rules is inapplicable to the new events. If this is the case, the agent is in a state of conflicting experience, those of the model conflicting with those of the mental map. The result is a gradual reclassification of the linkages and new rules are re-established (Hayek 1952: 119; Fleetwood 1995: 117). It takes a long period of time for the process to be completed. This reclassification process which triggers new rules is the foundation of understanding transition. A transition economy, in the subjectivist perspective, is thus defined as the situation where its people's current interpretation framework is outdated and is unable to cope with the rapidly changing external world. At the same time, a new framework for interpreting new events or solving new problems has not yet fully developed in their minds. As a result, a mental gap occurs. In other words, peoples' interpretation framework is in a vacuum state. This framework vacuum is transition.[111]

8.6 The process of transition: from perception to market selection

Although transition is a state of chaos, it does not mean that economic activities in transition economies are in standstill. On the contrary, transition should be viewed as a dynamic process of which people are struggling to re-establish a new interpretation framework. In this section, we try to explore what will happen during the process of transition or more precisely, how 'the act of reclassification' leads to the change in the society's stock of knowledge and consequently, re-establishes new institutions. To do so, we utilize the Hayek's theory of spontaneous order (1967).

Actors' subjective interpretation of incoming events and the choice of an option are subject to social tests. Social selection in economic perspective, analogous to natural selection in biology, consists of three parts: variation, selection, and retention.[112] Variation occurs through human agency. Selection in the economy operates over objects that vary from time to time by rules or paradigms and through the realization of cost and benefit. Through filtering processes, those whose chosen option happens to lead to benefits will be weeded in. Otherwise, those whose chosen option happens to lead to losses will be screened out. Self-interest governs social selection. Once new ways of doing things are found to be feasible, people will use them repeatedly. In other words, these rules are adopted. As mentioned,

[111] Thus, my subjectivist perspective of transition is consistent with Hare's view (2001: 80). He describes transition economies as the economies where important institutions have not been created and that the relevant laws are incomplete, imperfectly enforced or still subject to serious political controversy.

[112] In biology, organisms were traditionally regarded as the objects of selection. Recently, genes become the main objects of selection. Variation occurs in each generation. It implies that the array of objects present at any time is heterogeneous. Some objects can adapt the current environment better than others and therefore will have more 'successes'. They are more likely to be 'selected' by the system whereas others will be more likely to be rejected. Greater fitness traditionally implied (probabilistically) differential reproductive success. Today, fitness is given by Hamilton's concept of 'inclusive fitness'. Retention is memory. In order to survive, selected variations must persist somehow. Retention is achieved mostly through genes (Langlois and Koppl 1994).

rules are the device for coping with our ignorance. They facilitate decision-making in complex situations. By trial and error, learning and experimenting, new rules emerge and serve as a new stock of knowledge. A dynamic theory of transition is thus based upon the conceptualization of processes of perception, experimentation and social learning. From this subjectivist perspective, we are now able to say something about the length of the transition period. Firstly, the deeper culture and social knowledge are embedded, the longer time agents will need to unlock old systems and therefore, the longer the transition period will be. In the case of which culture is so deeply rooted, moderate reform package to enhance unlearning or change may be rendered ineffective. Thus, a more radical approach is required to unlearn. Such radical approach may take in the form of political revolution and violence which are unavoidably painful and bloody. Secondly, the longer time it takes for people to interpret external events, unlearn obsolete knowledge and learn new things, the longer the transition period will be. This argument can be evidenced by the fact that the EU accession countries[113] learn faster than most Commonwealth of Independent States (IMF 2001: 165). The reason is essentially a problem of mental perception, classification and learning. Those nations which are closer to EU and therefore with significant understanding of a market-based economy will learn the western style of market system faster. In contrast, most of the CIS countries have no obvious alternative model to follow. With almost 70 years of central planning, these CIS nations have little knowledge of the operation of a market-based economy and therefore learnt new capitalist way of doing things in a much slower pace.

8.7 The future of transition economies: a journey into the unknown

Where are these transition economies heading? For most neoclassical and new institutional scholars, the answer is towards a market economy. In fact, most policy makers including the staffs of IMF and the World Bank believe that these economies should develop a form of western style of market economy. For IMF (2001: 175), 'building effective market-economy institutions is central to long-term growth prospects in all countries, but is particularly relevant for the transition economies, given the inadequacy of their pre-transition institutional arrangements'. Hence for IMF, the

[113] The EU has accepted ten transition economies as full candidates. They are Bulgaria, the Czech Republic, Estonia, Hungary, Latvia, Lithuania, Poland, Romania, the Slovak Republic and Slovenia (IMF 2001: 178; see also Veugelers and Mrak 2009: 9).

role of the government in the transition economies should transform from direct intervention in economic activities to an agency involving in the establishment and enforcement of the 'rules of game' (IMF 2001: 174). Moving towards a western style of market economy is only one of many possible destinations. In fact, as Hare (2001: 78) points out, some of the transition economies may not even wish to transform themselves into market-type economies. In our subjectivist perspective, the answer is that these economies do not necessarily move to the western style of market economies nor return to previous communist regimes. Instead, they take on a journey into the unknown. This is the essence of Austrian evolutionism.

According to Carl Menger, there are two types of institutions, namely designed and undesigned.[114] While both are created by human agents, they differ in one essential way, namely if they were anticipated or unanticipated. The former type arises because of common will directed toward its creation and the result is more or less anticipated. The latter is 'the unintended result of innumerable efforts of economic subjects pursuing individual interests' (Menger 1883[1985]: 158). It is the unanticipated consequence of purposive human action. A striking feature of the Austrian theory of transition is that human agents are creating a system which they do not know in advance. Though in a sense of being human-made, that is, the result of economizing actions, institutions are largely not designed, nor the intended product of these actions (Hayek 1979: 147). In fact, Hayek contends that human agents are creating something they *never* know, not to mention whether the emerging systems are efficient or not. In Hayek's words (1979: 150),

> 'many of the greatest things man has achieved are the result not of consciously directed thought, and still less the product of a deliberately coordinated effort of many individuals, but of a process in which the individual plays a part which he can never fully understand'.

[114] Based on Carl Menger, Langlois (1986) argues that institutions can be pragmatic or organic. Pragmatic institutions comprise rules directed toward specific ends. Conscious intentions play an important role if the institution is not very complex and confined to a relative short time perspective, so that the original intentions of the founder can influence the shape of the institution. However, institutions can also be the unintended consequence of human action. The rules of thumbs operating evolve over time into an institution that no one has expected to emerge, although it is the result of the human economizing effort.

This argument sharply contrasts with the new institutional belief that human institutions are constructed as a result of the maximization of human choice under constraints. Rather, they are the result of a long-term evolutionary process of learning, creating and experimenting. For this, Weisskopf notes (1997: 309-327):

> 'What is striking is that, in a number of important spheres, the economic reforms have worked out in a different way than initially intended... popular values and expectations rooted in Russian culture have reacted to the shock therapy reforms in such a way as to generate a new economic situation that is neither a normal Western-style capitalist system nor a traditional Soviet-style socialist system'.

In Peter Earl's words (1998), transition economies are 'heading for a journey into the unknown'. Assisted by IMF or World Bank, these transition economies may attempt to move to the western style of market economies but they are indeed evolving into something that no one knows, just like the time when human agents created the astonishing communist regime in 1917.

8.8 Resistance of change during the transition period

It is reported that resistance of change occurring in Russia in recent years due to the dramatic fall in the output. Suffering from poverty in the chaotic economy, some Russians wish to return to the 'good old days' of the communist regime. To explain the resistance of change, new institutional economists emphasize on transaction costs and capabilities.[115] Public Choice school emphasizes on rent seeking activities.[116] For Cheung (1982: 34-36), institutional change depends on two types of transaction costs: the costs of operating the system (costs of delineating and policing rights, negotiating and enforcing contracts), and the costs of institutional change encompassing costs such as discovering alternative institutions or persuading people to adopt change.[117] In Cheung's view, the broader the

[115] For a capabilities explanation of institutions and inertia, see Langlois and Robertson (1995: 102-112).

[116] For public choice scholars, adherence to reform trap is attributable to rent seeking activities. To escape the under-reform trap, Aslund *et al.* (2001: 88-108) suggest to induce competition to break monopoly.

[117] Langlois and Robertson (1995) refer to the costs of discovery, persuading, and teaching other market participants as 'dynamic transaction costs'.

range of methods or techniques for making production decisions is, the lower the cost of production will be. Cheung (1982: 40-41) concludes that the relative lack of institutional choice under communism means that the costs of operating the system are necessarily higher than those in a private enterprise system. His arguments imply that if the cost of discovering alternative institutions or persuasion is relatively high, then existing institutions will persist.

In the evolutionary literature, persistence of institutions is largely explained by the concept of path dependence which suggests that lock-in effects and inefficient behaviors may persist and that history matters in explaining institutional deficiencies (Arthur 1989; David 1995).[118] Path dependence plays an important role in North's adaptive efficiency framework. For North, the complementarities, economies of scope, and network externalities bias change in favor of the interests of the existing organizations. In his view (North 1992: 12):

> 'the interests of these existing organizations, which produce path dependence, and the mental models of the entrepreneurs, which produce ideologies, rationalize the existing institutional matrix and therefore bias the actors in favor of policies conceived to be in the interests of existing organizations'.

Our subjectivist perspective casts light on institutional inertia or resistance of change during transition. Persistence of an old system is fundamentally associated with mental thinking. As mentioned, the society's total stock of knowledge is a product of mental interpretation, reclassification and learning. Agents' interpretation process has a certain time sequence that allows thinking to follow a routine perception track. In other words, agents see things in a certain way and expect things to be worked out in a certain way. Once the incoming information is organized into a (mental) pattern, then the agents' subjective interpretation framework no longer has to analyze or categorize incoming information. All that is required is to have enough information to trigger the pattern. The mind then follows along the pattern automatically in the same way as a driver follows a familiar road. Over time, a habit develops because the actor simply uses his or her interpretation system routinely. Resistance to change means that actors' thinking is locked up in old interpretation structures, concepts and institutions (DeBono 1992: 17). Two further points are worth to

[118] For a discussion of the effect of path dependence on the transformation of Central European countries, see Chavance and Magnin (1997).

mention. Firstly, once agents take the stock of knowledge for granted, then perception becomes even more important, because the way they look at a situation will determine what they can do about it. Secondly, unless another competing pattern is developed in the agent's interpretation framework, anything similar to the established pattern will be treated just as if it were that pattern. It is just like the watershed to a valley. Unless there is a competing valley, water will gather into the centre of the single valley. Furthermore, when economy's stock of knowledge is seen as a product of social construction, rules or moral norms are then followed relatively unconditionally since the behavior prescribed by them is considered 'right'. If individuals act against these rules, then they will have a 'bad conscience'. Hence, an institution is reinforced during the process of socialization when individuals learn to behave according to the 'right' rules of the game that constitute the society they live in (Ackermann 1998).

It may be argued that in order to prevent institutional inertia and accelerate transition process, whenever interpreting incoming events is necessary, actors should not take their experience or knowledge for granted. Unfortunately, as Allen and Haas (2001: 25) notes, all psychological change is very hard to bring about. It is often the case that individuals are unwilling to let go of existing concepts, perceptions or institutions in order to put both previous and recent experiences into a new perspective. As explained above, rule-following has its merits. After a period of time, as the pattern in agents' minds survives for too long, it will become non-separable and resisted disruption. In other words, over time each piece of knowledge works together, forming an integrated part of the thinking pattern, and is reinforced by social norms, customs and routines. By that time, changing patterns will become extremely difficult (DeBono 1992: 17). This is the case of North Korea. Unless there are Schumpeterian innovations which revolutionize the way of doing things, old thinking will persist as long as agents take experiences for granted unconditionally and interpret the external world in a routine manner.

8.9 Two routes of economic reform: 'gradualism' versus 'shock therapy'[119]

If we accept the argument that economic transition is a matter of change in mental perception, then our framework can shed light on the

[119] Due to limitation of space, my application here can only be illustrative. Further research along this line of reasoning is called for.

understanding of two types of reform, namely gradualism, denoted by the reform in Mainland China and the shock therapy, denoted by the reform in Russia. Gradualism is notably incremental in nature. In the 1980s, the Chinese government steadily introduced the economic reform. Rather than admitting the acceptance of capitalism, the Deng government subtly termed the reform as modernization, or 'adoption of a market system under socialism'. This gradual reform policy had one advantage. Chinese people could partially maintain their old thinking while at the same time learn new ways of doing. Starting in the agricultural sector, the government de facto introduced a private property rights system under the name of 'agricultural responsibility system'. This new policy served as a small impulse to the peoples' minds. Innovative opportunities began to be perceived by farmers and rural workers. At first, farmers did not know what to do. During that time, they were still using the same old interpretation framework to deal with new events. Many of them dared not to move ahead. This was especially true for those people who suffered intense hardship during the Cultural Revolution. With socialist thinking being still in force in most farmers' mind at the early stage of the reform, those people moving ahead and behaving as rural entrepreneurs were condemned by other farmers as capitalists' devils. However, as many rural entrepreneurs became wealthy and had not suffered from any political condemnation, old thinking started to give way. As more farmers learned, new policies were found feasible. More precisely, Chinese people slowly constructed a new framework to deal with the capitalist way of doing things. Such mentality gained ground and was reinforced by continuous rewards. With the success in the rural sector, similar reforms were then extended to the industrial sector under the name '*Bao Chan Dao Hu*' (a contracting system).[120] More and more people accepted the new way of doing things. Even most conservative communist cadres were later willing to unlearn and learn. They had given up their radical communist ideology. They participated in the market ways of doing things and involved in private enterprises. A new social stock of knowledge has been steadily built up as these activities are extended to the whole economy. Chinese people are now able to interpret new global events without much difficulty. As they share the same expectation, economic activities in China can be coordinated at relatively lower costs. This explains the success of China's reform.

Contrary to the gradualist approach, the shock therapy (or big-bang strategy) requires people to give up entirely all their existing stocks of

[120] Many types of contracting systems were practiced during the experimentation period. For a detailed discussion, see Shiu (1997).

knowledge at one time. Actors totally unlearn old ways of doing things and learn new things in a very short period of time. This involves revolutionary learning.[121] In Russia, It means that people abandoned all communist teaching which they had taken for granted for many years and accepted capitalists' ways of doing things.[122] This had created a shock in the mental process. The Russians suddenly found that their stocks of knowledge were incapable to solve their daily problems. In other words, shared expectation disappeared. Coordination failed. As a result, production and economic activities were in chaos. This explains the fact that in transition economies of Central and Eastern Europe, the Baltics, Russia, and the other countries of the former Soviet Union, output fell by more than 40% on average. Such real output loss was accompanied by severe dislocations, large redistribution of income, and severe income losses by many people (Fischer 2001).

Given the dramatic fall in the output and suffering from extreme hardship during the reform, a lot of Russians with their old interpretation framework being still in force in their minds may perceive that it is easier to cope with everyday life under the communist system than in the transition stage. Therefore, some of them started to miss their good old Bolshevik days. Their minds still strongly valued economic stability and desired security under the communist regime (Weisskopf 1997: 309-327). This explains why some Russian resisted the economic reform. To reiterate, a successful economic reform requires a change in mentality. After all, a human institution is not 'an objective physical phenomenon, but a human mental construct' (Stein 1997: 730). On this, a policy reform package aims to help people to learn new things are of utmost important.

8.10 Conclusion

The Austrian approach presented in this chapter represents an alternative to social engineering approach prescribed by the mainstream neoclassical school and property rights perspective articulated in the evolutionary institutional paradigm. The subjectivist approach attempts to understand

[121] Revolutionary learning can be seen as 'a process of deinstitutionalization or unlearning in which anomalies with established knowledge embedded in structural principles and properties are discovered' (Stein 1997: 737).

[122] An old way of thinking is a strong desire for equal distribution of income. Another example is speculation. Speculation was also regarded as a criminal activity and was condemned. On the other hand, in Commonwealth of Independent States countries, no living memory of a market economy remains. For a review of old ways of thinking, see Allen and Haas (2001: 12).

transition and institutional change in the theory of human action. It starts with humanist elements including perception, learning, errors, expectation and experimentation, and extends the subjectivist analysis to economic phenomena in transition economies. In this way, understanding transition has its arguments firmly rooted in human agency. So far, the subjectivist approach to understand transition and institutional change is rare and this chapter provides only a schematic explanation of some transition issues. Further subjectivist research in transition is called for.

References

Ackermann, R. (1998) Institutional Path Dependence, History and Reform. Paper presented at the EAEPE Annual Conference in Lisbon, Portugal, 5-8 November 1998.

Allen, M. and R. Haas (2001) The Transition in Central and Eastern Europe: The Experience of Two Resident Representative. In: *Transition Economies: How Much Progress.* IMFstaffpapers, volume 48, Special Issue. Washington DC, USA: IMF, pp. 9-28.

Arthur, W.B. (1989) *Increasing Returns and Path Dependence in the Economy.* Ann Arbor, USA: University of Michigan Press.

Aslund, A., P. Boone and S. Johnson (2001) Escaping the Under-reform Trap. In: *Transition Economies: How Much Progress.* IMFstaffpapers, volume 48, Special Issue. Washington DC, USA: IMF, pp. 88-108.

Chavance, B. and E. Magnin (1997) Emergence of Path Dependent Mixed Economies in Central Europe. In: A. Amin and J. Hausiner (eds.) *Beyond Market and Hierarchy: Interactive Governance and Social Complexity.* Cheltenham, UK: Edward Elgar, pp. 196-232.

Cheung, S.N.S. (1982) An Economic Theory of Institution Change. In: *Will China go 'Capitalists'?* Hobart paper no. 94. London, UK: Institute of Economic Affairs, pp. 30-47.

Colombatto, E. (2002) Is There an Austrian Approach to Transition? *Review of Austrian Economics,* vol. 15 (1), 61-74.

David, P.A. (1995) Clio and the Economics of QWERTY. *American Economic Review,* vol. 75, 332-237.

DeBono, E. (1992) *Serious Creativity.* New York, USA: Harper Business.

Denzau, A.T. and North, D.C. (1994) Shared Mental Models: Ideologies and Institutions. *Kyklos,* vol. 47 (1), 3-31.

Earl, P. (1998) Consumers Goals and Journey into the Unknown. In: M. Bianchi (ed.) *The Active Consumer: Novelty and Surprise in Consumer Choice.* London, UK: Routledge.

Fischer, S. (2001) Ten Years of Transition: Looking Back and Looking Forward. In: *Transition Economies: How Much Progress*. IMFstaffpapers, volume 48, Special Issue. Washington DC, USA: IMF, pp. 1-8.

Fleetwood, S. (1995) *Hayek's Political Economy: The Socio-economics of Order*. London, UK: Routledge.

Hare, P.G. (2001) Institutional Change and Economic Performance in the Transition Economies. In: *Economic Survey of Europe*, no. 2. New York, USA: Economic Commission for Europe, United Nations, pp. 77-95.

Havrylyshyn, O. (2001) Recovery and Growth in Transition: A Decade of Evidence. In: *Transition Economies: How Much Progress*. IMF staffpapers, volume 48, Special Issue. Washington DC, USA: IMF, pp. 53-87.

Hayek, F.A. (1952) *The Sensory Order*. Chicago, USA: University of Chicago Press.

Hayek, F.A. (1962) Rules, Perception and Intelligibility. *Proceedings of the British Academy*. vol. XLVIII, 321-344; reprinted in F.A. Hayek (1967) *Studies in Philosophy, Politics and Economics*. New York, USA: Clarion Book, pp. 43-65.

Hayek, F.A. (1964) Kind of Order in Society. *New Individualist Review*, vol. 3 (3), 3-12.

Hayek, F.A. (1967) *Studies in Philosophy, Politics and Economics*. New York, USA: Clarion Book.

Hayek, F.A. (1979) Purposive Social Formations. In: *The Counter-Revolution of Science*. Indianapolis: Liberty Press, pp. 141-152.

International Monetary Fund (2001) *World Economic Outlook*, May 2001. Washington DC, USA: IMF.

Kierzkowski, A. (1997) The Assessment: Economics of Transition in Eastern and Central Europe, *Oxford Review of Economic Policy*, vol. 13 (2), 1-21.

Kornai, J. (2000) The System Paradigm. In: W. Schekle, W-H. Krauth, M. Kohli and G. Elwert (eds.) *In Paradigms of Social Change: Modernization, Development, Transformation, Evolution*. New York, USA: St. Martin's, pp.111-33.

Langlois, R.N. (1986) Coherence and Flexibility: Social Institutions in a World of Radical Uncertainty. In: I.M. Kirzner (ed.) *Subjectivism, Intelligibility and Economic Understanding*, New York, USA: New York University Press.

Langlois, R.N. and R. Koppl (1994) When Do Ideas Matter? A Study in the Natural Selection of Social Games. *Advances in Austrian* Economics, vol. 1, 81-104.

Langlois, R.N. and P.L. Robertson (1995) *Firms, Markets and Economic Change: A Dynamic Theory of Business Institutions*. London, UK: Routledge.

Mantzavinos, C., D.C. North and S. Shariq (2001) Learning, Change, and Economic Performance. working paper, Max Planck Institute, Germany.

Menger, C. (1883[1985]) *Investigations into the Method of the Social Sciences with Special Reference to Economics*. New York, USA: New York University Press.

Menger, C. (1871/1994) *Principles of Economics*. Grove city, USA: Libertarian Press.

North, D. (1990) *Institutions, Institutional Change and Economic Performance.* Cambridge, UK: Cambridge University Press.

North, D. (1992) *Transaction Costs, Institutions, and Economic Performance.* San Francisco, USA: An International Center for Economic Growth Publication.

Popovic, D. (2001) Discussants' comments on Professor Hare's Paper. In: *Economic Survey of Europe*, no.2, New York: Economic Commission for Europe, United Nation, pp. 95-97.

Rizzello, S. (1999) *The Economics of the Mind.* Aldershot, UK: Edward Elgar.

Rizzello, S. (2000) Economic Change, Subjective Perception, and Institutional Evolution, *Metroeconomica*, vol. 51 (2), 127 -150.

Roland, G. (2001) Ten Years After ... Transition and Economics. In: *Transition Economies: How Much Progress.* IMFstaffpapers, volume 48, Special Issue. Washington DC, USA: IMF, pp. 29-52.

Roland, G. and T. Verdier (2000) Law Enforcement and Transition. Discussion paper, No.2501, July, London, UK: CEPR.

Shiu, G. (1997) Searching for Stones to Cross the River: The Micro-experimental Approach to Economic Reform – Lessons from China. PhD Thesis, Department of Economics, George Mason University, Fairfax, USA.

Stein, J. (1997) How Institutions Learn: A Socio-Cognitive Perspective. *Journal of Economic Issues*, vol. XXXI (3), 729-740.

Veugelers, R. and M. Mrak (2009) The Knowledge Economy and Catching-up Member States of the European Union. Report prepared for Commissioner's Potocnik's Expert Group, Knowledge for Growth, May 2009.

Weisskopf, T.E. (1997) Economics Without History: The Effort To Westernize The East. In: N. Aslanbeigui and Y.B. Choi (eds.) *Borderlands of Economics: Essays in Honor of Daniel R. Fusfeld.* London, UK: Routledge Press.

Yu, T.F-L. (1998) Economic Development in Latecomer Economies: An Entrepreneurial Perspective. *Development Policy Review*, vol. 16 (December), 265-280.

Yu, T.F-L. (1999) Toward a Praxeological Theory of the Firm. *Review of Austrian Economics*, vol. 12 (1), 25-41.

Chapter 9. Entrepreneurial strategies for small firms in latecomer economies

9.1 Introduction

The significance and performance of small enterprises in economic development is well documented (see for example, Berry and Mazumdar 1991; OECD 2009). Not only do large firms in general begin as small ones, but also regions specializing in high-technology products, such as Silicon Valley, frequently have high concentration of technologically-advanced small concerns. Small firms in the 'Third Italy' similarly operate at high levels of efficiency by international standards even when they employ lower levels of technology. Small firms also dominate the Asian Newly Industrialized Economies (NIEs) whose growth records have been among the best in the world during the 1960s-1980s. Specifically, the economic success of two Asian economies, namely Hong Kong and Taiwan has been largely attributed to the dynamics of small firms (Sit and Wong 1989; Liao and Kao 1995; Numazaki 1997; Chen 2000). Despite the significance of small firms, the origins of competitive advantages and growth strategies for small firms in the latecomer economies have never been critically examined. Traditional neoclassical price theories are able to indicate that the dynamics of small firms lie in their flexibility, adaptiveness and responsiveness. However, in economics literatures, merits of small firms are largely explained in terms of diseconomies of scale associated with the expansion of production. In recent decades, evolutionary theories of the firm, which synthesize transaction costs concepts, capabilities theories, strategic management and traditional industrial economics, have opened a brand new world in analyzing business enterprises (see Conner 1991; Foss, Knudsen and Montgomery 1995; Langlois *et al.* 2002). Utilizing these new theories, this chapter discusses the competitive advantages, survival and growth strategies for small firms in Asian latecomer economies. It begins by examining the resources owned by small firms and their associated competitive advantages. It then discusses the survival and growth strategies for small latecomer firms. The last section of the chapter gives concluding remarks.

9.2 Distinctive assets of a small latecomer firm

For small firms in the latecomer economies to be successful and coexistent with large enterprises overseas, they must possess some distinctive assets and capabilities. Hence, this study begins by examining those unique attributes or resources of small firms which allow them to sustain a competitive advantage (Monteverde 1997: 100). In the resource-based literature (for example, see Christensen 1996: 113), three general types of firm resources are identified: physical resources, financial resources, and intangible resources. Small high-tech firms in early industrialized nations may possess technologists, relatively sophisticated equipment and innovative entrepreneurship. However, most small factories in Asian latecomer economies often employ fewer than 50 unskilled workers and sometimes use some outdated machinery to produce low-value-added commodities for export. In terms of physical resources, these small firms own no 'strategic assets' (Kay 1993: 64), since unskilled labor and production plant can be easily acquired in the market. Perhaps the two most distinctive intangible assets possessed by small firms are entrepreneurship[123] and a simple capital structure.[124] These two assets contribute to the firm's competitive advantages manifested in entrepreneurial alertness, organizational flexibility and lower costs of coordination.

9.2.1 Entrepreneurial vision and alertness

In most cases, the owner of the small firm is also the entrepreneur-founder. Hence, the firm is heavily influenced by the entrepreneurial spirit. Kirzner (1973) argues that a unique feature of entrepreneurship lies in its 'alertness to hitherto unnoticed opportunities.' Once entrepreneurs discover profit opportunities, they will exploit them to their benefits. They proceed through their alertness to discover and exploit situations in which they are able to produce at lower prices and sell for high prices. Alertness implies that the entrepreneur possesses a superior perception of economic opportunity. It is like an 'antennae that permits recognition of gaps in the market that give little outward sign' (Gilad *et al.* 1988: 483). Teece *et al.* (1997: 509) argues that identifying new opportunities, organizing effectively and efficiently embracing them are generally more fundamental to private

[123]According to Christensen (1996: 113), human resources include experience, judgement, intelligence, and the insights of the leaders and workers in the firm. Since these resources are dependent on specific people and their skills, they are the most flexible resources.

[124] Yu (2005: 37-53) argues that the firm is a collection of capital resources. The complexity of the capital structure of a firm increases as vertical integration increases.

wealth creation than engaging in business conduct that keeps competitors off balance, raise rival's costs and excludes new entrants. Similarly, Yu *et al.* (2006) show that the dynamics of small manufacturing firms in Taiwan have been principally attributed to Kirznerian entrepreneurship. More importantly, entrepreneurial alertness (Kirzner 1973) and judgement (Knight 1921), which rely on the ability to process complex and incomplete information usefully in an intuitive way, are inherently non-contractible and inimitable (Langlois 1995: 83), thereby, contributing to a sustained competitive advantage for the small firm.

9.2.2 Simple capital structure and organizational flexibility

Apart from the entrepreneurial factor, another distinctive advantage of a small firm is its simple capital structure. A small firm possesses few assets. Paradoxically, a simple capital structure can become a form of competitive advantage. Little physical assets contribute to external flexibility for the organization.

Flexibility is often regarded as a significant source of competitive advantage of small firms. However, a comprehensive analysis of small firms' flexibility in the capabilities perspective is still lacking. Production needs flexibility in order to respond rapidly to internal and external developments. Flexibility is associated with organizational inertia that is the unavoidable consequence of specialized investment in physical assets and social structures. Organizations have cores which are very difficult to change relative to more peripheral elements (Rumelt 1995: 105). For a large corporation with a long history, its owners have made tremendous investment in physical and human capital (Winter 1986: 168-188). Such investments are of a highly specific and irreversible nature and become the organizational routine. To these owners, the investments are also a sunk cost. Past irreversible investments yield continuing benefits that sustain old methods. Hence, adopting a new method renders high opportunity cost for large firms. On the contrary, simple capital structure associated with the small firm renders lower opportunity cost for the entrepreneur if change in the direction of production is required.

9.2.3 Lower internal communication costs

Arrow (1974: 56) argues that 'learning the information channels within a firm and the codes for transmitting information through them is indeed a skill of value only internally'. Within the firm, the most straight forward source of synergy is the learned ability of the team to communicate in dialect among one another, taking for granted a shared understanding of firm-specific routines (Nelson and Winter 1982). An organization's unique set of communication codes represent the idiosyncratic asset upon which a firm may build sustainable competitive advantage (Monteverde 1997: 99).

Coordination within a firm renders significant transaction costs that influence organizational forms. In general, small firms have better personal links, more unified culture and hence stronger identity. These features make communication easier (Kogut and Zander 1996: 502-518). Compared to large firms, owners of small firms are more prone to employ staff with whom they can share similar knowledge and culture, and thus make communication easier. In particular, small family firms tend to hire family members and adopt nepotism. This practice has the merits of reducing communication costs.

9.2.4 The role of charismatic entrepreneurship in corporate governance

There is still another corporate advantage for a small firm, namely, lower monitoring costs. The opportunistic version of transaction costs economics can easily indicate that fewer personnel in a firm can promote organizational efficiency by reducing transaction costs. For example, confidentiality of information is easier to guarantee if it is a matter of keeping it in the small team. However, the argument that employing small number of members can facilitate organizational efficiency lies to a lesser extent in lower monitoring costs, as suggested by the incentive or governance perspective of the firm. Rather, it is associated with the charismatic entrepreneur. As Witt (1998: 161-177) argues:

'a persuasive business conception adopted by an employee may detract her/his attention in a self-reinforcing manner from non-compliance alternatives that actually exist. Hence if the entrepreneur can dominate the informal communication process within the firm so that elements of her/his conception become tacit cognitive commonalities among the firm members, this may enable the entrepreneur to get the employees cognitively involved into her/his endeavor'.

Hence if a small firm relies heavily on the charismatic entrepreneurs who pose a parental image to their employees, such leadership will convince the members to comply with the goals of the firm. When employees feel that they are part of the company, they will less likely undertake opportunistic actions. Moreover, these employees may even engage in creative acts that are beneficial to the firm. Only if members consider themselves as outsiders will they exhibit opportunistic behavior.

9.3 Survival strategies for a small Asian latecomer firm

Given some competitive advantages of a small firm, namely, entrepreneurial alertness, organizational flexibility, lower transaction costs in communication and monitoring, we now can discuss some survival strategies of a small firm during its early stage of development.

9.3.1 Strategic entrepreneurship

As mentioned above, small firms are highly associated with entrepreneurial alertness. More importantly, given limited resources and technological base, small firms have larger chance of survival by pursuing guerrilla entrepreneurial strategies. Guerrilla entrepreneurship can be regarded as a significant business strategy for latecomer firms to compete with multinational giants. Small enterprises, with high flexibility, can exploit market opportunities by using guerrilla strategies. These firms seek out an opportunity for high profit margins in a particular good, develop a formula, and exploit it by rapidly flooding the market before the established firms can respond. They make profits over the short term, and then leave the market for another before competition forces prices down to the point where they are no longer profitable without large-scale investments in technology or infrastructure. Guerrilla entrepreneurial strategies are said to be essential to the industrial development of Asian latecomer economies such as Taiwan and Hong Kong. Most small entrepreneurial firms in these economies were able to survive in the global competition mainly by adopting guerilla strategies (Yu *et al.* 2006).

Jacobson (1992) argues that flexibility is a critical strategic factor in the entrepreneurial discovery process. To survive in global markets, firms must be ready to move into new lines, to alter their production plans and even to switch technologies at short notice. There is no room for inertia. In particular, in the electronics industry, it is reported that the average product life cycle for most of the electronic goods was approximately 18 months. If producers react slowly, they risk being left with stockpiles of unsold items (Wilson 1991: 38). Therefore, only by grasping new opportunities and making decisions quickly can small firms in latecomer economies continue to survive. For this reason, small latecomer firms should adopt a short-term view of production and maintain flexibility in order to adapt quickly to changing market conditions.

9.3.2 Imitation and strategic follower

During the initial stage, due to a low level of absorptive capacity[125] (Cohen and Levinthal 1990) and poor technological bases, small latecomer firms can conduct replication or imitation. Having noticed a product or a business pattern successfully launched by other produces, small firms can duplicate the activities at significantly lower labor and rental costs (and hence sell at lower prices). In other words, small firms conduct pure arbitrageurship on the (factor) price discrepancies. This replication activity is also named as 'pattern multiplication' (Vesper 1990: 6). In order to imitate successfully, these small firms need to be alert to opportunities, flexible and adaptable to the changing environments. Entrepreneurs of these establishments need to keep themselves informed of developments in innovating economies and quickly adopt their advances for themselves (Baumol 1988: 89).

Among various replication methods, reverse engineering is commonly adopted by small entrepreneurial firms in their early stage of catching up. Entrepreneurs of small latecomer firms can travel abroad, participate in international trade fairs and subscribe to professional journals for the purpose of searching opportunities for replication (Dahlman and Nelson 1995: 105). After identifying a target, they may arrange to obtain a license to duplicate the product at home. Some of them may simply buy a unit of the new product and conduct reverse engineering. Given that firms cannot afford to purchase a license from original suppliers, which are common for small firms, then closer scrutiny of how to produce the goods is impossible.[126] Yet, imitative firms are not directly concerned with creating a good likeness, but with achieving an economic success – preferably, an economic success at least equal to that of the original. Unlike innovative firms which can enjoy a monopoly situation, at least for an initial period,

[125] Cohen and Levinthal (1990: 128) defines absorptive capacity as 'the ability of a firm to recognize the value of new, external information, assimilate it, and apply it to commercial ends'.

[126] According to Nelson and Winter (1982: 123), there are two cases of copying, namely cooperative and non-cooperative. Cooperative copying can be either a joint venture, subcontracting or licensing. Non-cooperative copying means that the imitator cannot directly observe the original production process. When a problem arises in copying, it is not possible to resolve it by closer scrutiny of the original.

small imitative firms face keen competition from other similar firms in the industry, and therefore have to be very efficient in production. Rapid response is crucial for their survivals.

At the survival stage, small imitative firms do not aspire to leap-frog nor attempt to keep up with innovators. Instead, they follow way behind their technological leaders. In other words, replication or imitation is strategic follower (Freeman 1982: 179; Hagedoorn 1989: 91; Bolton 1993: 32). The imitative strategy should not be downgraded as non-creative (Bolton 1993). At the initial stage, producers have to imitate and compete on low labor costs. Furthermore, being a follower is less risky. Normally, replication occurs when the market becomes established and the original venture has been accepted. As the market segments become clear, marketing research can easily analyze the consumption patterns of customers. Bolton (1993: 32) shows that Matsushita's low-cost strategy in the consumer electronics business was built upon being a second-mover. The company deliberately arrived late in the marketplace, waited and watched until the consumers accepted a rival's new product, then started to produce a large volume of standard products which were sold at lower prices.

9.3.3 International subcontracting and OEM businesses

Multinationals from advanced nations often look for cost-reduction opportunities. In other words, these international giant firms conduct spatial arbitrageurship. Instead of establishing a subsidiary firm in developing nations, which may raise costs and introduce risks due to cultural barriers, these multinational firms use subcontracting method. In the international outsourcing arrangement, foreign firms often supply technical guidance, working capital, and even leased equipment to the firms in developing countries (Dahlman and Nelson 1995: 93). In this way, small local firms can take the opportunity to learn and imitate. One specific form of international subcontracting is called Original Equipment Manufacturer (OEM) in the electronics business,[127] in which small firms in latecomer economies produce according to the requirements of the orders received from overseas multinational giants. Products made by manufacturers in latecomer economies are sold overseas under the brand names of the multinational corporation (Ting 1985: 80; Hobday 1995:

[127] The term OEM was originated in the 1950s by computer manufacturers who used subcontractors (called the OEM) to assemble equipment for them. It was later adopted by US chip companies in the 1960s which used OEMs to assemble and test semiconductors (see Hobday 1995: 1190).

1178). This form of international subcontracting activity is significant for the small firms in Asian latecomer economies. For example, in Hong Kong, despite growth in design skills of some local firms, OEM businesses still account for a large proportion of total electronics output (Hobday 1995: 1176).[128]

The strategy of OEM business is best summarized by the statement: 'We (latecomer firms) make them; you (multinational corporations) sell them' (Yu 2003: 52-53). There are several advantages to act as an OEM supplier. Firstly, this strategy shuns grand marketing plans and multi-million-dollar brand promotions (Chiu and Lui 1993). Manufacturers save huge marketing expenses in promoting the brand. They let their foreign partners bear most of the risk of sale fluctuations.

Secondly, they save huge R&D expenses. For example, in the mid-1970s, among the Asian Newly Industrializing Economies, Hong Kong virtually spent nothing on R&D. Singapore and Taiwan spent about 1% of GNP on R&D, with the bulk of the R&D funded by the government, while South Korea spent only 0.5% of GNP on R&D (Dahlman and Nelson 1995: 107).

Thirdly, as OEM suppliers, they can seek assistance or advice from overseas firms (buyers) if difficulties arise (Hobday 1995: 1177). Several studies show that many foreign firms give detailed technical assistance to their subcontractors on how to organize production (Dahlman and Nelson 1995: 105).

9.4 Strategies for growth

Though small firms may survive at their initial stage of development, it does not mean that they can take the situation for granted forever. Globalization changes scenario rapidly. Small firms constantly face competition in the market. Therefore, they need to learn or acquire new skills in order to maintain competitive advantages. Any recommendation on growth strategies should base on the principle that economic change is evolutionary (Nelson and Winter 1982) and that learning and innovation are largely incremental. Radical growth strategies often bring about a disastrous result for the firm.

[128] For a detail discussion of the role of OEM in latecomer technological learning, see Hobday (1995).

9.4.1 Incremental rather than radical innovation to enhance competitive edges

To compete and expand, small latecomer firms cannot rely on pure replication strategies. In other words, sheer imitation cannot sustain growth. Firms must improve their products and sell them at low prices. As capabilities improve, small firms no longer limit themselves to those sectors where cheap labor has an obvious advantage. They also must look for profit opportunities through the introduction of improved products and the utilization of more sophisticated technology from overseas. Learning by doing (Arrow 1974) and learning by imitating (Bolton 1993) are crucial in this regard. Learning theories suggest that human cognitive systems are able to process, code and store information in the memory so that they will be available on subsequent occasions if needs arise. But the use of information depends upon the situation that prompts individuals to anticipate that a certain kind of performance will lead to reinforcement (Phares 1988: 353). Thus, cognitive systems can respond to the stimulus via a discrimination network. Although some people make naive responses when they organize their memories, many possess multi-dimensional, stimulus-discrimination networks and are able to make sophisticated responses (Hedberg 1981: 7).

Hence, the phenomenon in which small latecomer firms catch up with first-movers can be explained by the fact that entrepreneurial learning and imitation can lead to innovation. During the imitation process, small manufacturers pick and choose from different models and later combine them into a novel product. This means that imitators are no longer 'copycats' but innovative producers using the examples of others. At first, producers may struggle to imitate the contents of a certain product. But gradually they take a portion of a design from another product, and copy a little of the styles or functions of some others. Ultimately, this mixture becomes a single unique product scarcely recognizable as an imitation at all (Phares 1988: 353). This learning theory suggests that innovations are incremental rather than discontinuous. All 'new' knowledge are built upon previous experiences. Firms undertaking research in radial innovation and attempting to frog leaping others innovative firms often find themselves end up in severe financial troubles.

9.4.2 Towards specialization: the 'no-brand-one-niche-product' strategy

Depending on capabilities backgrounds, some small latecomer firms can choose to become manufacturing specialists in the service of product developers. Rather than diverting resources in product technologies, they concentrate on improving their manufacturing capabilities in the latest process technologies that yield the best performance as governed by the market. This strategy is that a latecomer firm concentrates on becoming the supplier of specialized niche components. In this regard, the latecomer firm needs to constantly invest resources in process innovation to stay at the production frontier. To do so, latecomer firms need to focus on improving their operational performance. This can be done either through obtaining the latest process technologies available from external suppliers and incorporating them into production as soon as possible to reap the advantage of being an early adopter, or through in-house R&D to develop their own process know-how. Besides working closely with leading equipment and component suppliers, firms also need to keep close contact with customers to anticipate future process requirements and to jointly develop customized solutions.

This strategy has several merits. Apart from avoiding the risk of commercializing new products, firms can prevent potential conflict of interest between themselves as manufacturers and buyers, thereby strengthening the loyalty of the buyers towards them. The ability of the process specialists to continuously innovate their production methods depends critically on the relationship with their end buyers. Only a close interaction with their customers enables them to gain intimate insights into current and future product requirements of their customers. Such supplier-buyer trust is difficult to develop if the customer perceives that the supplier poses a threat to vertically integrate forward in the future (Wong 1999).

9.4.3 Moving partially to Original Design Manufacturer (ODM)

As mentioned, entrepreneurs will discover that they are able to learn from multinational corporations that have taken the advantage of low production costs in developing areas (Engardio and Gross 1992: 67). For some long-term partners involved in the OEM business, overseas buyers may only provide a general idea of product requirements and leave the specific design to the OEM suppliers. If foreign buyers are satisfied with the finished products, this indicates that the OEM suppliers in latecomer economies can manage to produce independently. It is quite possible that the OEM suppliers may later launch similar products under their own brands and compete with the foreign firms that originally employ them. In other words, they can perform Original Design Manufacturer (ODM). However, we observe that most small firms in Asian latecomer economies simultaneously manufacture products that bear the labels of foreign firms (customer label products or OEM) as well as products that bear their own company labels (private label product or ODM). The reason is not difficult to understand. Producing and promoting private label products is too risky and too costly though the business has a higher profit margin.[129] On the other hand, customer label products involve less risk but have a lower profit margin, as argued in the previous section. A combination of the two represents a balance of the costs and benefits of the two kinds of labels. In short, movement away from a customer label product strategy towards a private label product strategy is an indication of improvement in firm's capabilities.

9.4.4 Provide sophisticated regional coordinators

The conventional thinking argues that firms must and should upgrade their technological bases on their way to expansion. However, we observe that many latecomer firms do not adopt offensive technological strategies. In particular, technological bases of many manufacturing firms in Hong Kong, Singapore and Taiwan are not upgraded even though these firms gained higher production capabilities. This phenomenon seems to contradict the conventional wisdom. However, careful investigation may help us to clarify this contradiction. There are many kinds of technological knowledge. Upgrading hardcore scientific or engineering technologies is only one alternative. Apart from this knowledge, there are managerial skills involving marketing, distributing, packaging and servicing. Therefore, rather than upgrading their hardcore technological bases, firms can utilize their skills which their capabilities or competitive advantages lie. The technologies that latecomer firms possess are not in hardcore engineering or science

[129] If firms sell products without promoting their brands, this means that they attempt to gain customers through very low prices. However, the profit margin is slim. On the other hand, if they promote their own brands, then consumers' confidence in the product is the major concern. To gain customers' confidence, imitators in developing countries follow closely the design style and the packaging of other successful branded products from overseas and try to avoid the locally-made image. For instance, they may use a German name for their brand-name. They strive to promote a high quality and a high class image for their products similar to those manufactured from the technologically advanced nations.

but in managerial skills and coordination. Therefore, instead of upgrading their hardcore scientific technological base, they can provide sophisticated managerial services to overseas firms. Specifically, these firms possessing global knowledge they learn from international subcontracting can now serve as regional coordinators between western advanced firms and firms in developing economies.

After receiving contracts from foreign buyers, local latecomer firms now equipped with international business skills can subcontract some parts or all of the production processes to other firms in developing areas. By relocating or subcontracting labor-intensive activities to the low costs regions, while keeping offices in home office as coordinating centers, these manufacturing firms gradually develop into international trading firms. In extreme cases, some firms might have no production site in their hometown at all. They simply maintain an office for administrative purpose and subcontract all jobs to other factories from the orders they received. They now specialize in venture creation, international marketing, outsourcing, and co-coordinating. They earn rewards by providing their managerial and marketing knowledge to foreign buyers and sellers.[130] Hence, these firms in a modern form serve as coordinators of transnational production (Yeung 1998: 8).

9.5 Conclusion

Utilizing transaction costs concepts, capabilities theories, strategic management, evolutionary and entrepreneurial economics, this chapter has discussed the competitive advantages of small Asian latecomer firms. It argues that entrepreneurial alertness and judgement are important strategic assets of a small firm because entrepreneurship is inherently non-contractible and inimitable. Furthermore, a simple capital structure of a small firm contributes to organizational flexibility. Facing uncertainty and volatile external situation, small firms, without investing too much in specialized assets and with only ad hoc routine, are able to minimize the influence of inertia and make a quick response to change. When entrepreneurs perceive that the old routine has to be completely abolished, the cost of closing down a small firm is much lower than the large firm counterpart. In this way, organizational flexibility of small firms implies industry capabilities.

[130] For an account of such international coordination by a Hong Kong company, see Berger and Lester (1997: 39-41).

This chapter also discusses and recommends some survival and growth strategies for small firms in other latecomer economies based on the principle that economic change is evolutionary. During the initial stage of development, small latecomer firms can survive by conducting guerrilla entrepreneurship, imitation and follower strategies, and involve in international subcontracting as Original Equipment Manufacturers. Through learning and imitation, small firms later can conduct incremental innovation. As capabilities grow, these firms may move towards specialization, adopting 'no-brand-one-niche-product' strategy. Some of them can also partially move to become an Original Design Manufacturer. Finally, depending on their technological bases, some firms can serve as regional coordinators, by providing managerial, sourcing, international marketing and outsourcing services in the global markets.

References

Arrow, K.J. (1974) *The Limits of Organization.* New York, USA: Norton.

Baumol, W.J. (1988), Is entrepreneurship always productive? In: H. Leibenstein and D. Ray (eds.) *Entrepreneurship and Economic Development.* New York, USA: United Nations, pp. 85-94.

Berger, S. and R.K. Lester (eds.) (1997) *Made by Hong Kong.* Hong Kong, China PR: Oxford University Press.

Berry, A. and D. Mazumdar (1991) Small-Scale Industry in the Asian-Pacific Region. *Asian Pacific Economic Literature,* vol. 5(2), 35-67.

Bolton, M.K. (1993) Imitation versus innovation: lessons to be learned from the Japanese. *Organizational Dynamics,* vol. 22, 30-45.

Chen, C.H. (2000) Organizational Capability and Bandi: Economic and Social Transformation in Taiwan. Society for the Advancement of Socio-Economics, 12th Annual Meeting on Socio-Economics, UK, London, 7-10 July 2000.

Chiu, S. and T.L. Lui (1993) Industrial restructuring in Hong Kong: Implications for production and employment strategies. Conference Paper, Centre of Asian Studies, University of Hong Kong, 11 October 1993.

Christensen, J. (1996) Analysing the Technology Base of the Firm: A Multi-dimensional Resource and Competence Perspective. In: N.J. Foss and C. Knudsen (ed.) *Toward A Competence Theory of The Firm.* London, UK: Routledge, pp. 111-132.

Cohen, W.M. and Levinthal, D.A. (1990) Absorptive capacity: A new perspective on learning and innovation. *Administrative Science Quarterly,* vol. 35, 128-152.

Conner, R.K. (1991) A Historical Comparison of Resource-Based Theory and Five Schools of Thought within Industrial Organization Economics. *Journal of Management*, vol. 17, 121-154.

Dahlman, C.J. and R. Nelson (1995) Social absorption capability, national innovation systems and economic development. In: B.H. Koo and D.H. Perkins (eds.) *Social Capability and Long-term economic growth*. New York, USA: St. Martin Press, pp. 82-122.

Engardio, P. and N. Gross (1992) Asia's high-tech quest. *International Business Week*, vol. 30 (November), 64, 67.

Foss, N.J., C. Knudsen and C.A. Montgomery (1995) An exploration of common ground: Integrating evolutionary and strategic theories of the firm. In: C.A. Montgomery (ed.) *Resources in an Evolutionary Perspective: Towards a Synthesis of Evolutionary and Resource-Based Approaches to Strategy*. Boston, USA: Kluwer, pp. 1-17.

Freeman, C. (1982) *The Economics of Industrial Innovation*. 2nd edition. London, UK: Frances Pinter.

Gilad, B., S. Kaish, and J. Ronen (1988) The entrepreneurial way with information. In: S. Maital (ed.) *Applied Behavioural Economics*, Vol. II. Somerset, UK: Wheatsheaf, pp. 481-503.

Hagedoorn, J. (1989) *The Dynamic Analysis of Innovation and Diffusion: A study in Process Control*. London, UK: Pinter Publisher.

Hedberg, B. (1981) How organisations learn and unlearn. In: P.C. Nystrom and W.H. Starbuck (eds.) *Handbook of Organizational Design Volume 1: Adapting Organisations to their Environment*. Oxford, UK: Oxford University Press, pp. 3-27.

Hobday, M. (1995) East Asian latecomer firms: learning the technology of electronics. *World Development*, vol. 23 (7), 1171-1193.

Jacobson, R. (1992) The Austrian School of Strategy. *Academy of Management Review*, vol. 17 (4), 782-807.

Kay, J. (1993) *Foundations of Corporate Success*. Oxford, UK: Oxford University Press.

Kirzner, I.M. (1973) *Competition and Entrepreneurship*. Chicago, USA: University of Chicago Press.

Knight, F.H. (1921) *Risk, Uncertainty, and Profit*. New York, USA: Houghton Mifflin.

Kogut, B. and U. Zander (1996) What Firms Do? Coordination, Identity and Learning. *Organisation Science*, vol. 7 (5), 502-518.

Langlois, R.N. (1995) Capabilities and Coherence in Firms and Markets. In: C.A. Montgomery (ed.) *Resources in an Evolutionary Perspective: Towards a Synthesis of Evolutionary and Resource-Based Approaches to Strategy*. Boston, USA: Kluwer, pp. 71-100.

Langlois, R.N., T.F-L. Yu and P.L. Robertson (eds.) (2002) *Alternative Theories of the Firm*, 3 volumes (The International Library of Critical Writings in Economics Series). Cheltenham, UK: Edward Elgar.

Liao, H.C. and C. Kao (1995) The Development of Small and Medium-Sized Enterprises in Chinese Taipei. In: E.Y. Park (ed.) *Small and Medium-Sized Enterprises and Economic Development*. Seoul, South Korea: Korea Development Institute.

Monteverde, K. (1997) Mapping the Competence Boundaries of the Firm: Applying Resource-based Strategic Analysis. In: H. Thomas, D. O'Neal and M. Ghertman (eds.) *Strategy, Structure and Style.* West Sussex, UK: John Wiley.

Nelson, R.R. and S.G. Winter (1982) *An Evolutionary Theory of Economic Change.* Cambridge, USA: Harvard University Press.

Numazaki, I. (1997) The Laoban-Led Development of Business Enterprises in Taiwan: An Analysis of the Chinese Entrepreneurship. *Developing Economies*, vol. 15 (4), 440-457.

OECD (2009) *OECD Small and Medium Enterprise Outlook*, 2009 Edition. Paris, France: OECD.

Phares, E.J. (1988) *Introduction to Personality*, 2nd edition. London, UK: Scott, Foresman and Co.

Rumelt, R. (1995) Inertia and Transformation. In: C.A. Montgomery (ed.) *Resources in an Evolutionary Perspective: Towards a Synthesis of Evolutionary and Resource-Based Approaches to Strategy.* Boston, USA: Kluwer Academic Publishers, pp. 101-132.

Sit, V. and S-L. Wong (1989) *Small and Medium Industries in an Export-Oriented Economy: The Case of Hong Kong.* Hong Kong, China PR: The Centre of Asian Studies, University of Hong Kong.

Teece, D.J., G. Pisano and A. Shuen (1997) Dynamic Capabilities and Strategic Management. *Strategic Management Journal*, vol. 18 (7), 509-533.

Ting, W. (1985) *Business and Technological Dynamics in Newly Industrialising Asia*. London, UK: Quorum Books.

Vesper, K.R. (1990) *New Venture Strategies.* revised edition. Englewood Cliffs, USA: Prentice Hall.

Wilson, J. (1991) It's Do or Die for a Struggling Chip Industry. *Electronics Business Asia*, July, 71.

Winter, S. (1986) The Research Program of the Behavioural Theory of the Firm: Orthodox Critique and Evolutionary Perspective. In: B. Gilad and S. Kaish (eds.) *Handbook of Behavioural Economics* (Vol. A). Greenwich, USA: JAI press.

Witt, U. (1998) Imagination and Leadership: The Neglected Dimension of the Evolutionary Theory of the Firm. *Journal of Economic Behaviour and Organisation*, vol. 35 (2), 161-177.

Wong, P-K. (1999) National Innovation Systems for Rapid Technological Catch-up: An Analytical framework and a Comparative Analysis of Korea, Taiwan and Singapore. Paper delivered at the DRUID Summer Conference on National Innovation Systems, Industrial Dynamics and Innovation Policy, Rebild, Denmark, 9-12 June 1999.

Yeung, H.W-C. (1998) *Transnational Corporations and Business Networks: Hong Kong Firms in the ASEAN Region*. London, UK: Routledge.

Yu, T.F-L. (2003) Guerrilla Entrepreneurship and Hong Kong's Economic Dynamics. In: Yu, T.F-L. (ed.) *East Asian Business Systems in Evolutionary Perspective: Entrepreneurship and Coordination.* New York, USA: Nova Science.

Yu, T.F-L. (2005) *Firms, Strategies, and Economic Change: Explorations in Austrian Economics*. Cheltenham, UK: Edward Elgar.

Yu, T.F-L., H-D. Yan and S-Y. Chen (2006) Adaptive Entrepreneurship and Taiwan's Economic Dynamics. *Laissez-Faire*, vol. 24-25, 57-74.

Chapter 10. Conclusion

10.1 Introduction

Ever since Carl Menger, the founder of the Austrian school of economics, views economic problems in subjectivist perspective, economic subjectivism has gone through several major transformations via the works of Ludwig von Mises, Friedrich A. Hayek, Israel M. Kirzner, Murray N. Rothbard and Ludwig M. Lachmann. In particular, Von Mises brings subjectivism to a milestone by integrating the methodologies of Max Weber and Alfred Schutz into his theory of human action. When economic enquiry comes to F.A. Hayek, the discipline does not deal with physical objects anymore, as positivism does, but with ideas and intentions. As Hayek (1955: 25) puts it, 'the objects of economic activity cannot be defined in objective terms but only with reference to a human purpose goes without saying. Neither a commodity nor an economic good, nor food or money can be defined in physical terms but only in terms of views people hold about things.' Furthermore, subjectivism in economic analysis has made significant contribution to our understanding of human action. Hayek (1955: 31) claims that 'it is probably no exaggeration to say that every important advance in economic theory during the last hundred years was a further step in the consistent application of subjectivism.' This book follows the Austrian economics tradition and view issues of economic development in subjectivist lens.

10.2 Understanding economic development in subjectivist lens

This book has started with a review of theories of economic development in history of Austrian economics (Chapter 1). Though major scholars in the Austrian school of economics such as Carl Menger, Eugene von Bohm-Bawerk, Ludwig von Mises, Fredrick A. Hayek and Israel M. Kirzner did not focus their analysis on development issues, it is possible to distil some of their views associated with the causes of economic progress of a nation. Austrian economists always explain the market and development processes in light of uncertainty and knowledge problems. Given that economic problems are coordination problems, they argue that entrepreneurship plays significant role in economic development and central planning is unable to boost economic development. They conclude that government interventions through taxation or regulations will in general hamper economic growth.

After reviewing theories of economic development in Austrian economics, this volume has proposed a human agency approach to economic problems in general and economic development in particular (Chapter 2). Based largely on the works on Max Weber, Alfred Schutz and Ludwig von Mises, a theory of subjectivist interpretation has been developed in this volume and applied to various aspects of economic development including entrepreneurship, national capabilities, innovation, trade, government policy, transition and catching up strategies for latecomer economies.

Entrepreneurship is said to be the engine of economic growth. However, the entrepreneurial process has rarely been discussed in the development literatures. This book has presented a dynamic model of the entrepreneurial process (Chapter 3). It argues that human agents experience as they make sense out of their everyday business life. Experiences from everyday life are accumulated into a stock of knowledge that can be used to interpret incoming events as well as problem solving. If incoming events are repeated and familiar, the entrepreneur can utilize the rule of thumb to solve problems without difficulties. If incoming events are novel, the entrepreneur's interpretation framework will fail to give an adequate account of the new situation. Encountering this situation, some agents may continue to use old methods to solve new problems. This response does not catch up with the market's expectation and is doomed to fail. Most entrepreneurs will devise new methods to solve new problems by trial and error, and experimentation. They will cope with their knowledge-deficiency by creating temporary expectations. This knowledge surrogate will be later tested in the market. If the new strategy works, then it will be adopted and further routinized as a rule of thumb. Moreover, human agents do not only passively adapt to the external environment but also subjectively define their futures. Using their imagination, they create an environment to which they will adapt via experimentation, learning, trial and errors. Entrepreneurs' imagination and projections are again subject to market tests. If plans do not meet expectations in the market, this implies that entrepreneurs have committed errors in planning. Given divergent tastes and expectations and rapidly changing world, each entrepreneur must exercise judgment. Judgment is liable to err. Wrong judgment or mistake in planning means that entrepreneurs' plans are unable to meet the expectations of other people. The whole entrepreneurial process is thus seen as a process in which the interpretation framework is corrected, adjusted, or refined. Business success is the result of correct entrepreneurs' judgment on the market. In conclusion, profit and loss, originating from uncertainty, serve as signals for entrepreneurs to interpret and re-interpret market phenomena and allows the ideas of market participants to coordinate.

Economic progress of a nation depends on its learning and innovative capabilities. This book constructs a theory of national capabilities from the subjectivist perspective (Chapter 4). Using the 'first person' perspective, this article starts from the level of individual human agency and explains economic capabilities based on the theory of human action. This subjectivist perspective is then extended and applied to the firm in relation to national capabilities and competitiveness. While the influence of institutions on firms' decision making is recognized, the subjectivist perspective, unlike contemporary evolutionary literatures, highlights the fact that all institutions represent the coordinating effort of human agents, who attempt to interpret external events or make sense out of social or economic interactions. The subjectivist perspective on national capabilities developed has been used to explain some important issues in development economics.

Innovation has been a significant issue in economic development. Many developing countries attempt to modernize via technology upgrading. One important aspect of economic management is the adoption of technology. This book seeks to explain the acceptance of an innovation or a novel idea from a phenomenological perspective (Chapter 5). It argues that whether a new idea is accepted or not by the community is a matter of subjective interpretation. This concept of intersubjective understanding has been used in this book to explain how innovative works are interpreted and accepted by the community. The phenomenological approach to understand an innovation in artwork is illustrated by oil paintings of Pablo Picasso. Implications regarding different types of innovations (namely, radical breakthrough versus adaptive innovation and scientific innovation versus art creativity) in association with their community's acceptance are discussed.

The mainstream neoclassical international trade theory exhibits many weaknesses and problems. Hitherto, scholars in Austrian economics have extended their criticisms on many aspects of the mainstream neoclassical theories including methodology, development economics, monetary theory, public finance and comparative economic systems. Little has been said on the pure theory of international trade. This volume attempts to fill this gap and suggests a new direction of research agenda (Chapter 6). Specifically, we have also adopted the Schutzian theory of human agency in understanding international trade. This subjectivist approach emphasizes on how human agents in the global market interpret world economic conditions, and make judgments and decisions under the genuine uncertainty. Elements in Austrian economics such as entrepreneurial learning, experimentation and innovation are incorporated in the economic analysis of international trade. It concludes that the Austrian subjectivist approach, if further applied to international finance, can contribute tremendously to various global issues such as new international economic order and globalization.

Government plays an important role in economic development. However, unlike most Austrian economists who reject all forms of government intervention, my research attempts to understand political agents' behavior and the decision making process in the public sector. Chapter 7 has incorporated cognitive elements such as opportunity discovery, learning, experimentation, trial and error, and revision of plans to understand a policy change. It argues that, given genuine uncertainty, political agents perceive external events, formulate plans according to their experience and knowledge. With new information and experience, they subsequently revise their plans in order to eliminate errors. Unlike neoclassical public economics, our perspective suggests that the impact of a government policy on the economy is not deterministic. Instead, many government policies yield a surprise to the economy and result in policy change. It is concluded that both agents in the private and public sectors cruise into the journey of an unknown future.

Despite growing literatures on economics of transition in recent years, the concept of transition is still very much in poverty. In this book (Chapter 8), we have provided a new perspective of transition. It puts forward a subjectivist theory of transition which attempts to understand transition and economic change in terms of the theory of human action. This approach focuses on humanist elements including perception, learning, expectation, errors, experimentation and creativity. Extending the subjectivist analysis to economic phenomena, this chapter concludes that each of transition economies will head for a unique system that no one knows in advance. This framework will shed light on two important issues: (1) the resistance of change during the transition period and (2) on the debate between two types of reforms, namely, 'gradualism' and 'shock therapy'.

Policy makers and development economists are always interested in searching policies which can enhance growth of developing countries. In evolutionary perspective, this book (Chapter 9) has provided a growth strategy for latecomer economies through promoting small business firms. It argues that entrepreneurship and simple capital structure are two major distinctive assets of small firms. These two assets provide small firms with competitive advantage manifested in entrepreneurial alertness, flexibility and lower costs of coordination. During the initial period of development, small firms in developing economies with low absorptive capabilities would survive by pursuing guerrilla entrepreneurship, imitation and strategic followership, and involve in international subcontracting as original equipment manufacturers. Through learning and imitation, small firms can later conduct incremental innovation to enhance competitiveness. As capabilities grow, depending to their technological bases, some of these firms may move towards specialization using one-niche-no-brand product strategy or partially move towards an original design manufacturer. Others may even serve as regional coordinators in the global market, by providing managerial services, sourcing, international marketing and business consultancies to foreign sellers and buyers. This chapter concludes that successful experiences of small firms in Asian latecomer economies can be a useful lesson for small businesses in other developing countries to compete and grow in global markets.

Our subjectivist approach has provided new insights in economic development. Having said that, other school of thought or approaches can be complementary to our subjectivist paradigm in explaining economic change. In particular, insights from public choice school, new institutional school and evolutionary economics are consistent with and useful to our subjectivist approaches. Combining insights from these paradigms with our Austrian subjectivism can open up a new direction in research into economic development.

10.3 Public Choice School: understanding government in economic development

Ever since founded by James Buchanan, the Public Choice School has developed into two streams: namely neoclassical Public Choice School and subjectivist Public Choice School. The former uses neoclassical optimization method to study the government, while the latter, in original Buchanan's flavor, understand the government in the subjectivist perspective. Austrian economics share similar outlook with subjectivist Public Choice School. The affinity between Austrian and subjectivist Public Choice School is most obviously seen in the approach to cost. Buchanan has made it clear that subjective cost theory is a crucial element in his work in public choice and public policy. In his little but important book *Cost and Choice* (1969[1999]), Buchanan states that '[c]ost is subjective, it exists in the mind of the decision-maker and nowhere else ... Cost cannot be measured by someone other than the decision maker because there is no way that subjective experience can be directly observed' (Buchanan 1999: 41). In contrast, mainstream economists generally treat cost as an objective measure and can be estimated ex post by external observers.

Buchanan also shares with the Austrians the latter's rigorous application of methodological individualism in economic research. As Public Choice economist Thomas DiLorenzo points out, '[t]he idea that the individual should be the unit of analysis has spared public choice and Austrian economists from many of the mistakes of what might be collected economics' (DiLorenzo 1990: 189). Through his insistence on constructing economic arguments from individual acts, Buchanan is able to pinpoint the futility of building welfare economics upon the existence of a social welfare function and treat government as an institution through which collective activities are being carried out rather than an actor itself as in traditional public finance.

Austrian economists' deep skepticism towards the ability of government in imposing particular outcomes in markets is also shared by Buchanan and the Public Choice School. To the Austrians, disperse knowledge and the impossibility of officials to get their hands on such knowledge renders any action beyond laying the ground rules for cooperation on the part of the government dubious. Public Choice economists, on the other hand, see officials as self-interested individuals pursuing their own interests rather than public ones. The Austrians and the Public Choice economists thus proffer complementary arguments challenging governmental actions built upon officials' circumscribed knowledge ability and the incentives they face respectively.

10.4 New institutional economics: institution and economic development

From the beginning, Austrian economists accept the view that institutions matter in economic development and incorporate institutional analysis in their works (Koppl 2005). For example, Carl Menger's theory of the evolution of money is the classic illustration of an Austrian theory of institutions. New institutional economics (NIE) also tries to explain the emergence, evolution, and significance of the underlying institutional order in which market processes operate. According to Ebeling (2007: 94), some of the new institutional scholars (e.g. Kasper and Steit 1998; Furubotn and Richter 1998) have consciously incorporated elements of the Austrian perspective in their theories. A good example can be found in the work of one of the founding members of the New Institutional Economics, Oliver Williamson (1975, 1985). Austrian economists view the market as an ongoing process rather than a state of affairs. Analyzing how the market process unfolds is thus one of the central questions Austrian economists attempt to answer (Kirzner 1992). Indeed, one can also trace an element of process analysis in Williamson's theory of why vertical integration exists in economic change. According to the Williamsonian theory of vertical integration, trading hazards exist when a transaction involves specific investments unique to the particular transaction in question. In such a situation, one of the trading partners in the transaction may act opportunistically and extract surplus from the other trading partner making the specific investments. Vertical integration thus serves as a means to eliminate such transaction hazards. Notice the process element inherent in this particular Williamsonian theory. Before a commitment has been made by the trading partner who has to make the relation-specific investments, he or she has many potential trading partners to choose from. Hold-up problem, therefore, does not arise. However, once a contract is signed and investments made by one of the trading partners in the transaction, the two parties are then locked into in a bilateral relationship instead of a multilateral one. Exit becomes costly for the trading party who has made the relation-specific investments and opportunity for the other party to extract surplus arises.

10.5 Evolutionary economics: history matters in economic development

The approach of Austrian economics can be regarded as evolutionary. Menger (1883[1985]: 10) claims that 'as many individuals act, the effects of their action are seen to comprise elements that no single individual ever contemplated and that were never contemplated by individuals acting in concert since there was no concert to begin with'. Although Austrian scholars recognize the significance of culture, social norms and institution in economic analysis, they refuse to accept historical determinism, as put forward by Marxist, Historical or older Institutional Schools. Instead, Austrian economists always recognize the creative power of human agency. However, people create the future that they do not know in advance (Hayek 1979: 150). A new idea or innovation has to go through the market test. Profitability is the criterion market uses to select winners and losers. Through filtering processes, those new ideas happen to lead to profits will be accepted. Those happen to lead to losses will be eliminated or phased out. Once new ways of doing things are found profitable or feasible, others will start imitating the successful few who brought the new ideas to the market place in the first place. On the other hand, new ways of doing things which resulted in losses would serve to dissuade others from adopting them. Such is the way through which effective means of doing businesses are spread while unsuccessful ones discarded in the market process. More importantly, people learn and accumulate experiences from the continuous process of experimenting with new ideas. These experiences and learning serve as the cognitive foundation upon which businessmen formulate their next new business ideas. Once new methods of conducting businesses are proven in the market place and before new ones introduced, people will use continue them until displaced by latter ones. When sufficient number of market participants adopts similar means to go about doing their businesses, such as choosing corporate form of organization rather than say partnership, those means become institutions.

In summary, this book has outlined a subjectivist approach to economic development. It is worth noting that if we combine our subjectivist approach with insights from public choice school, new institutional school and evolutionary economics, research in economic development will be more fruitful than what we can have from the mainstream neoclassical paradigm.

References

Buchanan, J.M. (1969[1999]) *Cost and Choice: An Inquiry in Economic Theory.* Indianapolis, USA: Liberty Fund Inc.

DiLorenzo, T.J. (1990) The Subjectivist Roots of James Buchanan's Economics. *The Review of Austrian Economics*, vol. 4, 180-195.

Ebeling, R.M. (2007) Austrian Economics and the Political Economy of Freedom. *New Perspectives on Political Economy*, vol. 3 (1), 87-104.

Furubotn, E.G. and R. Richter (1998) *Institutions and Economic Theory: The Contribution of the New Institutional Economics.* Ann Arbor, USA: University of Michigan Press.

Hayek, F.A. (1955) *The Counter-Revolution of Science: Studies on the Abuse of Reason*. Glencoe, USA: The Free Press.

Hayek, F.A. (1979) Purposive Social Formations. In: Hayek, F.A. (ed.) *The Counter-Revolution of Science*, Indianapolis, USA: Liberty Press, pp. 141-152.

Kasper, W. and M.E. Steit (1998) *Institutional Economics: Social Order and Public Policy.* Northampton, USA: Edward Elgar.

Kirzner, I.M. (1992) *The Meaning of Market Process.* London, UK: Routledge.

Koppl, R. (2005) Austrian Economics at the Cutting Edge. Paper for the Annual Meeting of the Society for the Development of Austrian Economics, 19 November 2005, Washington DC, USA.

Menger, C. (1883[1985]) *Investigations into the Method of the Social Sciences with Special Reference to Economics.* New York, USA: New York University Press.

Williamson, O.E. (1975) *Market and Hierarchies.* New York, USA: Free Press.

Williamson, O.E. (1985) *The Economic Institutions of Capitalism.* New York, USA: Free Press.

Keyword index

G

H

I

J

K

L

M

N

O

P

R

S

T

U

V

W